CITIZEN-SOLDIER: OPPORTUNITIES IN THE RESERVES

by
Carl White, Major USMC (Ret.)

ROSEN PUBLISHING GROUP, INC.
New York

Published in 1990 by The Rosen Publishing Group, Inc.
29 East 21st Street, New York, NY 10010

First Edition

ISBN-08239-1023-7

Library of Congress Cataloging-In-Publication Data

White, Carl.
    Citizen-soldier : Opportunities in the Reserves /
by Carl White
        p.   cm.
    Includes bibliographical references.
    ISBN 0-8239-1023-7
    1. United States—Armed Forces—Reserves.
I. Title.
UA42.W46   1990
355.3'7'0973—dc20
                                                89-48814
                                                CIP

Manufactured in the United States of America

About the Author

Carl White retired as a major in 1980 after more than twenty years in the U.S. Marine Corps. He had completed eight years of regular and Reserve enlisted service and had attained the rank of sergeant when he was selected to attend the Marine Corps' Officer Candidate School at Quantico, Virginia. Commissioned a second lieutenant in 1966, he later served in combat in Vietnam as an advisor to a South Vietnamese Marine infantry battalion. Other service included duty as commander of a U.S. Marine rifle company on Okinawa, advisory duty with a Marine Reserve unit in western Pennsylvania, and a number of other assignments with Marine and joint service commands around the world. Among personal decorations awarded for his military service are the Bronze Star with Combat "V," the Vietnamese Cross of Gallantry, the Joint Service Commendation Medal, and the Purple Heart.

Following his retirement from the Marines, White worked as a press spokesman for the U.S. State Department during the federal emergency that evolved when more than 125,000 Cuban refugees came to this country in 1980; later he became deputy director of the federal task force responsible for administering a major Cuban refugee center in Arkansas. He returned to his present home in northern Virginia in 1981 and became a founding partner of Media Services: Washington, an editorial consulting business that he now owns.

White has contributed numerous articles to consumer and defense-related publications, including *The Almanac of Seapower*, and was editor of *Government Executive Magazine* for two years. He is editor of a regional life-style magazine and is consulting editor for two annual publications on U.S. Reserve forces and the North Atlantic Treaty Organization.

Contents

Preface

The decision to enter military service is one of the most important decisions a person will ever make—whether for duty in the active forces or as a Reservist. It is, therefore, a move that should be undertaken only after thoroughly examining military life in general and, more specifically, the opportunities available in each of the armed services.

This book is intended to help in the decision-making process. It should be used in conjunction with visits to armed forces recruiting offices and discussions with parents and friends—especially friends who have served or are now serving in the active armed forces or the Reserves.

Members of the recruiting services can provide information about current programs and about the opportunities available at local Reserve units. They can also help in identifying and choosing military occupational specialties and, in some instances, in determining whether a person is qualified to enter highly specialized occupational fields.

It is often helpful for someone considering Reserve service to include others in discussions with recruiters—parents, spouse, or friends. They can sometimes bring up important questions that might otherwise be overlooked. In that regard, it is also usually helpful to write down questions before each meeting with recruiters.

Once the decision is made to enter Reserve service, a number of military requirements must be fulfilled before departing for active duty. These include certain written tests and a physical examination. As those processes take place, the service is verifying information provided by the applicant.

A medical condition or some other factor may disqualify an applicant for service or cause temporary disqualification. In any case, it is important for the service to be aware of any existing medical condition or previous serious ailment and for all administrative questionnaires to be completed as accurately as possible.

Once testing and physical examinations have been completed and an applicant is determined qualified for entry into service, he or she may depart immediately for active duty and basic training, or departure may be delayed for up to several months. Such delay may be for the convenience of the recruit or for the good of the service. For the recruit the delay may be in order to complete high school or other schooling or to meet civilian employment obligations. Delays for the convenience of the service may be in order to schedule a recruit for initial training in such a way that he or she will be able to enter a formal military school that begins at about the time basic training is completed.

Many types of specialties and training programs are available in each of the armed forces and their Reserve components. Additionally, new programs are constantly evolving, existing ones being discontinued, and others being modified. It should be noted that those described in this book were available at the time of writing but may since have been modified, replaced with another program, or eliminated. Armed forces recruiters are the best sources for up-to-date details on enlistment and commissioning programs, military specialty schools and training programs, pay and allowances, enlistment and reenlistment bonuses, and other options in their particular branch.

In discussing the armed forces and Reserve service with a recruiter, you incur no obligations. Should you feel that you are being pressured to enlist or enter a commissioning program, you should end the discussion and resume it only when you feel comfortable in doing so—preferably after discussing the matter with persons in whom you have confidence such as parents, teachers, or mature friends.

Armed forces recruiters are responsible for the sometimes

difficult task of helping to fill the ranks of their service with qualified people. The better qualified a young person appears, the more interested a recruiter is in seeing the applicant enter his or her branch of service. It is your responsibility in choosing to enter military service to do so freely and without mental reservation. In that regard, and to avoid the possibility of misunderstandings that could lead to problems after entry into service, any promises or guarantees made by a recruiter should be obtained in writing. The vast majority of recruiters for the U.S. Armed Forces are honest and honorable people; however, mistakes relating to promises and guarantees can be made. Fewer are made when details are in written form.

A major portion of this book relates actual events that have taken place during weekend and annual training and during special missions by Reserve units of the armed forces. The purpose of describing such events is to provide examples of the wide range of activities undertaken by young men and women who have responded to the needs of their country and at the same time taken advantage of opportunities to improve themselves—both physically and mentally—through national service.

Reserve service is challenging; however, it is more than equally rewarding. After reading this book, take a more detailed look by discussing with local recruiters the Reserve units in or near your own community. I'm confident you'll discover a new world of opportunity—very close to home.

Part 1

RESERVISTS—FULL PARTNERS IN A TOTAL FORCE

Chapter I

The Reserve Mission

Coaches of athletic teams often boost chances for success by loading their benches with "second-string" players who are as capable and competent as members of the first team. This strategy, the coaches say, adds "depth" and helps assure consistently strong performances against tough opponents. The U.S. Armed Forces, in fielding strong, well-trained, well-equipped Reserve Forces, use that same principle for developing depth and increasing the likelihood of victory over forces that might threaten America's national interests.

The U.S. Reserve Forces were once considered useful primarily for follow-on or reinforcing roles in the event of national emergency. Moreover, it was national policy to maintain small active forces during peacetime, with Reservists prepared to support them in the event of war. Today, Reservists play a much more prominent role in the overall scheme of America's national defense. Since the mid-1970s a concept called the "Total Force Policy" has, year by year and systematically, added to the peacetime responsibilities of the Reserves. Today, Total Force means heavy reliance on the reserve components, which are expected to perform as full partners in national defense both in peacetime and upon mobilization.

Whereas once Reserve and National Guard units were expected to be prepared to deploy from their home training centers in crisis situations in a matter of weeks or months, they now must be able to move out and into action in hours or days. (If moving out in a matter of days for some units seems slow, consider the large amounts of heavy equipment they routinely train with on drill weekends but would have to prepare for shipping to forward locations upon mobilization.)

The people training at local armories and airfields on "drill weekends" are a cross section of American society. They are our next-door neighbors. In a typical Reserve or National Guard unit are citizen-soldiers who in their civilian pursuits may be stockbrokers, local or state police officers, civil engineers, truck drivers, insurance brokers, service station attendants, computer programmers, homemakers, commercial airline pilots, hotel managers, or workers in just about any other occupation. For one weekend each month they meet as a military unit, train, and carry out the same types of military missions that their active force counterparts might perform. They also spend two weeks on active duty each year working as a unit, refining skills they have already developed and learning new ones.

They are paid for their Reserve service and receive other benefits and privileges available to members of the active forces, including entitlement to retirement pay for more than twenty years of service. Enlistment in the Armed Forces Reserve is by contract and carries an obligation to serve for a specified period of time; persons reenlisting after that initial term do so for varying periods of time, often with the objective of accruing enough service to qualify for retirement income. Persons accepting commissions as officers in the Reserve components accept a different set of obligations but have the same basic commitment to national defense.

In 1987 more than 265,000 young American men and women became members of the Reserve Forces.

The Reserve Components

As indicated in the following table, the Navy, Marine Corps, and Coast Guard each has a single Reserve component; the Army and Air Force each has two:

Active Force	*Reserve Component(s)*
U.S. Army	U.S. Army Reserve
	Army National Guard

Active Force	Reserve Component(s)
U.S. Air Force	U.S. Air Force Reserve
	Air National Guard
U.S. Navy	U.S. Naval Reserve
U.S. Marine Corps	U.S. Marine Corps Reserve
U.S. Coast Guard	U.S. Coast Guard Reserve

Each Reserve component has a primary mission of maintaining combat-ready units that are prepared to mobilize and deploy in support of national military needs whenever more units or personnel are required than are in the active component. Unlike the other services, the Coast Guard is not a part of the Department of Defense during peacetime. However, during wartime or at other times as the President directs, the Coast Guard and its Reserve serve in the Department of the Navy. Its Reserve personnel train and operate with the active Coast Guard and are prepared to join active force units on a full-time basis in the event of mobilization.

The Army National Guard and Air National Guard, in addition to maintaining combat-ready units, have secondary missions. They must be prepared to protect life and property and to preserve peace, order, and public safety under state authorities. For example, when a major hurricane threatened the Texas coast in 1988, the governor of Texas called members of the Texas Army National Guard to active service to assist with evacuation of coastal communities and provide security for homes and businesses in evacuated areas.

Operating in the Total Force

Since the mid-1970s the combined active and Reserve forces have come to be known as the Total Force. This simply means that America relies on all members of the armed forces—regulars and Reserves—to work as a team to assure national security. It also means that Reservists and National Guard personnel must often work shoulder to shoulder with members of the active components to assure that critical missions are accomplished—in peacetime situations as well as in armed conflicts.

In the recent past Air Force Reservists and Air National Guard crews participated in missions aboard aerial tankers that provided refueling support to U.S. aircraft during the bombing strikes against Libya in response to terrorist acts against American citizens. Naval Reservists served aboard minesweepers and other vessels when the U.S. Navy positioned ships in the Persian Gulf to protect shipping during the Iran-Iraq War. Naval Reservists also served aboard the battleship USS *New Jersey* when it was in the Mediterranean supporting American forces ashore in Lebanon in the early 1980s. Army Reserve civil affairs personnel assisted in restoring order in Grenada when the U.S. seized control of the island from Cuban forces and returned it to the island's own government. Air Force Reserve crews evacuated American students from Grenada in that same operation.

On an ongoing basis, Air National Guard pilots intercept Soviet aircraft just outside America's air defense zones; and Coast Guard Reservists routinely participate in drug interdiction and surveillance operations aboard active force aircraft and vessels.

Like the active force elements of the Total Force, each Reserve component draws its members from a number of sources. A person may join the Reserves directly through a recruiting office; enter as an officer through a Reserve Officer Training Corps (ROTC) program or other special program; or enter Reserve service after serving in an active component.

Just over 1.6 million men and women are serving in the Reserve components, which collectively are called the Ready Reserve. Most Reserve component personnel are assigned to units with which they meet and train a regular basis. They are members of the Selected Reserve. Just over 30 percent of Reservists, however, are not assigned to units but are members of the Individual Ready Reserve or Inactive National Guard—trained personnel who can be mobilized quickly if needed.

Senior executives of the Department of Defense determine

It is not uncommon for Americans to see motor convoys of Reserve and Guard personnel moving to and from nearby field training on weekends or more distant major military installations for two weeks of annual training duty.

the number of Reservists needed at any given time and, working with the President and Congress, establish the personnel strengths that can be funded for a specific fiscal year—the federal government's operating year, which runs from October through September 30 of the following year. Each Reserve component is then given the personnel strength level with which it is expected to operate during the year.

Reaching and sustaining the desired strength level is not always easy. In fiscal year 1987, for example, the Coast Guard could meet only 47 percent of its need for Selected Reserve mobilization personnel because of reductions in its budget. In that same year the other Reserve components operated at from 90 to 100 percent of personnel requirements.

Even when a Reserve component is operating at or near its desired strength, there may be severe shortages of personnel in certain occupational fields. In one recent year all of the Reserve components experienced shortages of 10 percent or more among enlisted personnel in some specialties.

Maintaining appropriate active and Reserve personnel strength levels consumes substantial amounts of money and time for all the services. Today's modern weapons systems and the administrative equipment needed to support them must be staffed by intelligent men and women capable of performing their duties effectively and efficiently. Normal attrition of personnel leaving the Reserve components after completing their period of obligated service, retiring after a Reserve career, or being discharged for a variety of reasons creates a demand for creative and aggressive recruiting programs among all the services. In 1987 that meant recruiting more than 250,000 men and women for Reserve service.

The perpetual cycle of people entering and leaving the Reserve forces also means a need for millions of dollars for basic military training and the specialty training to produce the special skills required in all fields, from the infantry to sophisticated missile operations. Because most enlisted Reservists serve on active duty for only six months, technical training continues at the local Reserve training sites one weekend each month and during at least two weeks of active duty each year.

For many Reservists, military specialty training and civilian occupational skills complement each other. Indeed, the training Reservists receive in military service often produces skills that lead to civilian jobs and careers. Many of the nation's civilian airline pilots and aircraft support personnel received their initial aviation training as Reservists; some of the leading computer authorities received their first exposure to computers during Reserve service; and the leadership skills gained during Reserve service frequently are carried over into the civilian workplace and help in career advancement.

The civilian career implications of Reserve training remain secondary, however, to the purpose of Reserve service— national defense preparedness.

Training

Reserve and National Guard units have taken on increasingly larger portions of America's national defense requirements over the past fifteen years. Whether practicing combat patrols in woodlands just a few miles from their hometown, flying aerial refueling missions thousands of miles at sea, or conducting many other activities during weekend drills or other periods of active duty, the primary responsibility of each Reservist is readiness. Readiness is attained through high levels of training designed to prepare individuals and units for smooth and rapid mobilization in the event national security is threatened.

Many of the jobs carried out by Reservists today were until recently considered solely the responsibilities of the active components. Additionally, Reserve units are expected to be able to perform primary mobilization missions rather than just serve as support or reinforcement for active units. This, in turn, creates a greater demand for training that is realistic, demanding, and focused on wartime missions.

The increased reliance on Reserve strength has led to replacement of many items of older equipment in the Reserve forces with military hardware with capabilities equal to that available to the active components. Certain Air Force Reserve and Air National Guard flying squadrons now maintain and operate advanced aircraft identical to those flown by some active force squadrons; certain Army, Navy, and Marine Reserve units are the only ones of their type serving the Total Force and in some cases operate equipment not available to their active component counterparts in peacetime. Since Coast Guard Reservists routinely fulfill their weekend drill commitments with the active Coast Guard, they must be fully qualified to operate the most advanced equipment and systems in service.

Specialty training at active component schools usually follows basic military training for enlisted Reservists. Course duration may be such that a Reservist may be able to serve a brief period of the initial six months' active service with an active component unit before returning home to begin service with a local Reserve unit. The type of training carried out with the unit at or near the Reservist's hometown relates directly to the unit's anticipated mission in the event of mobilization. A Marine Corps Reserve ground transportation unit in western Pennsylvania may spend a good part of its weekend training in trucks on mountain roads, improving driver skills and convoy techniques. Sailors with a Naval Reserve helicopter squadron may participate in practice minesweeping operations in the Chesapeake Bay. Army Reservists belonging to a light antitank battalion in California may spend some of their drill weekends in the field aboard major bases for live-fire training exercises.

Reserve communications specialists, computer technicians, supply personnel, and many other types of specialists meanwhile fulfill drill weekend obligations with units structured to support active force organizations with combat missions.

In addition to a two-day drill period each month, a Reservist is required to perform two weeks of active duty training annually. This training usually takes place with the hometown unit, which deploys to a major active component or National Guard base. But the two weeks of active duty is not always in the United States. The Department of Defense, in an effort to improve mobilization readiness and increase the realism needed for effective training, is now sending larger numbers of Reservists and Reserve units to overseas locations for annual active service. In 1987 nearly 95,000 Reserve and National Guard personnel trained in 84 nations.

In addition to the new emphasis on overseas deployment for training, added realism is being achieved by more joint exercises, which require Reservists and active force personnel from different services to coordinate their efforts in solving problems and carrying out missions just as they would have to do on a day-to-day basis in the event of war. Such training is used to advance individual and unit skills and test the overall readiness of personnel, equipment, and systems, and it often involves forces from other allied nations.

Training takes into account defense plans, which in some cases call for movement of Reserve units to frontline areas ahead of active component forces. Reservists must be well trained, well equipped, and well led for the jobs they will be asked to do. They are a major element in the formulation and execution of both foreign policy and national defense policy.

America's Reserve forces add depth to national security; however, they are no longer considered second-team players. They are first-team players serving at home.

Chapter II

The Commitment: Reserve Service Considerations

Service in the U.S. Armed Forces and their Reserve components offers many benefits—benefits that are provided by the American people, through their tax dollars, because of the great importance of military service to the nation. The benefits are not simply an indication of appreciation, however, but also a means of recognizing and rewarding persons for accepting the significant responsibilities undertaken by anyone entering military service. For Reservists those responsibilities are many, regardless of which component one joins or what one's military occupation may be.

When someone chooses to become a Reservist he or she must be prepared to participate in a structured and often demanding schedule, not just during the initial months of active duty but for the duration of service. In order for a Reserve unit to conduct realistic training on drill weekends and during annual training duty, it is important that as many members of the unit as possible attend scheduled training periods. Therefore, although alternate or makeup drill periods may be arranged in instances when a Reservist is unable to attend scheduled drill periods, such arrangements are generally discouraged. To perform as a team, a unit must train as a team.

Reserve unit leaders often plan drill weekends a year or more in advance and attempt to schedule them on the same weekend of the month throughout the year. This helps Reservists in their personal planning. For some units, however, such scheduling is impossible, and drill weekends may fall irregularly over the course of the year. In either case, Reservists must live with the fact that they are obligated to perform military duties for two days each month—in most instances, on a weekend.

Reservists and Civilian Employment

Another obligation incurred by Reservists is two weeks of annual training duty each year. Such duty is usually performed with the other members of the unit for consecutive weeks at a site far from the local Reserve training center—usually at a major military installation in the U.S. or in field training exercises abroad. Many civilian employers support their employees who are Reservists by not charging annual duty against vacation time. Many also allow work schedules to be coordinated around drill weekends. This is not always possible, however. Therefore, persons who are employed and planning to enter Reserve service should determine their employer's policies regarding Reserve training. Reserve service also must be taken into consideration by Reservists when they consider civilian job or career changes.

Many young men and women planning to enter Reserve service find that their employer or supervisor was once a Reservist or member of the active forces—or even is presently a Reservist. Such business leaders—as well as many with no history of military service—are often very cooperative as the potential Reservist plans and prepares for service. In some instances, however, a company's personnel policies, financial situation, or other factors may make it difficult for the supervisor or employer to be helpful.

As is described in a later chapter, a person entering the active forces or Reserve service has certain reemployment and job protection rights under law, which cover the extended periods of active service, including service during general mobilization. However, some employers may be unable or simply choose not to be cooperative about weekend drills and annual training duty. That is all the more reason for anyone planning to enter the Reserve forces to meet with employers and supervisors to discuss company policies regarding such service. Often Reserve unit leaders and Armed Forces recruiting personnel are available to discuss service obligations and responsibilities with a prospective Reservist's employer.

Almost every aspect of a person's family life is affected to some extent by Reserve service. Vacations, social events, business obligations, community service, religious activities, and other personal interests all must be considered with the military obligation in mind. As noted earlier, a Reservist may be permitted to miss some scheduled drills and make them up later, but such arrangements are not always practical or possible. This means that certain social or employment-related occasions may be missed by a Reservist over the course of his or her military service.

The number of Reservists who serve for twenty or more years, however, indicates that the impact of Reserve service on personal life is not an unbearable burden. Many career Reservists have weighed the impact of service on personal life against its benefits and decided that the inconveniences are not so great as to cause them to end their career before earning retirement benefits. And for many, the Reserve unit and the friends they make within the unit become important parts of their personal life.

The impact of Reserve service on family life varies greatly between Reserve units and, of course, often depends on the life-styles of individual Reservists and their families. In many instances, inactive duty for training—usually held in the form of weekend drills—is such that Reservists can return home on the evening between drill days. But for some units, especially aviation flying units and combat and combat support units, weekend drills are more commonly carried out at distant air facilities or field training sites. Those locations and the nature of training are such that it is often not practical or feasible for Reservists to spend evenings between drill days at home with their families. Sometimes families can travel to military bases that serve as annual training duty sites and arrange to stay on or near the base. However, such Reservists are not likely to be able to spend evenings or weekends with their family because of the amount of time they spend in field training or away from the base.

Reserve Training and College Classes

Anyone attending or planning to attend college and considering Reserve service must also consider the impact such service may have on their efforts to gain a higher education. Although Reservists today receive special benefits relating to education (which are discussed elsewhere in this book), weekend drills and annual training duty must be considered by a person developing an academic schedule for college semesters or quarters. Many times, but not always, coordination with Reserve unit leaders and college officials can resolve potential conflicts.

To a Reservist's advantage, however, is the fact that Reserve unit leaders encourage educational advancement and are always on the lookout for enlisted Reserve personnel who have earned associate and bachelor's degrees and may be qualified for Reserve commissioning programs. Sometimes being a full-time college student *and* a Reservist may be difficult, but the two can be compatible. Many of today's Reservists are carrying full academic loads at trade and technical schools, junior colleges, and four-year colleges and universities. Many are paying substantial portions of their education costs with pay earned from Reserve service and through service-related tuition assistance programs.

Training and Family

Monthly drill and annual training duty generally become a matter of routine over the course of a Reservist's military career. Dealing with part-time military service becomes a family affair. At some units Reservists and their families develop informal social groups and make lasting friendships with other members and their families. Such groups provide mutual support during annual training duty when many Reservists must travel to training sites without their families, and they are available to assist each other in the event a Reservist is called to active duty suddenly in a national or international crisis.

Responding to Crisis

Regardless of the reason or reasons a person may become a member of a Reserve component, the most important aspects of his or her service relate to peacekeeping and national mobilization. The Reserve forces are considered peacekeepers inasmuch as their presence serves as a deterrent to countries that might consider hostile acts against the United States. Foreign nations must be aware that America's standing regular forces are supported by a large, powerful, mobile, and rapidly responsive Reserve force. The presence of such a ready force serves as a powerful influence on any nation considering aggressive acts against the U.S., its citizens, or its interests abroad.

In addition to assuming a personal commitment to be a part of a peacekeeping effort, a Reservist also undertakes an even greater commitment—to take up arms immediately to support and defend the national interests of the United States in the event of war or impending war. The possibility of becoming personally involved in armed conflict or major international crisis may seem very remote most of the time, but international political situations and other factors influencing relations among nations can change rapidly. Such was the case in 1950 when North Korea invaded South Korea; substantial numbers of the American troops first transported to frontline combat positions were Reservists. They had been called to active duty and rushed to Asia while major active force units were being reinforced for sustained operations and prepared for later movement to the combat zone.

The possibility of general mobilization—a time when all Reservists are expected to go quickly to active duty—must become part of the Reservist's planning throughout the entire time of service. Reservists are encouraged by their unit leaders to work with their families, employers, business associates, and, if they are business owners, their employers and clients in developing plans for action if the Reservist is suddenly called to active duty. In some instances Reservists have been given several weeks' notice of being called to active duty; however, this has not always been the case, nor is it expected to be in the event of a major crisis requiring military power.

Reservists, therefore, must not only plan personal actions and life-style in light of the possibility of rapid mobilization, but must also keep their Reserve unit informed as to certain aspects of their personal life. Unit commanders must know at all times where and how to contact members of their unit. Unit administrative staffs must know the marital status and number of members in each Reservist's family, and how to contact family members at any time. Reserve medical staffs must know of any illnesses suffered by unit members in order to be able to treat them in the event of mobilization or determine that a member is temporarily or permanently not medically qualified for service. Reserve commanders need to know the civilian skills held by unit members—skills that might be called into use in the event of mobilization. Still other aspects of a Reservist's personal life either are essential or may be inquired about by unit leaders to make for a more ready and capable Reserve force.

Extended Peacetime Service

Participation in international crises by Reservists does not always involve mobilization. During tensions in the eastern Mediterranean and Middle East in the mid-1980s, Air National Guard crews flew refueling and resupply missions in support of active forces. During that same period, Air National Guardsmen and Reservists from the other services performed other important missions in those areas and other locations around the world where international tensions had developed.

Members of the Army National Guard and Air National

Guard are in a unique position in that they are subject to be called to active service on very short notice by the governor of their state in situations such as the aftermath of natural disasters.

It is the "mobilization factor," however, upon which all else in Reserve service is centered. The skills and capabilities of each member are measured and tested continually, considered with the skills and capabilities of all other members of the unit, and used in determining overall readiness of the unit for mobilization. Testing usually is carried out on the unit as a whole, but individual proficiency examinations are also used to help evaluate unit readiness and determine ability to function as a member of the Reserve team.

Qualifications for promotion also involve testing and are another matter that often impacts on a Reservist's personal life. Inasmuch as drill periods often entail field training or other activities involving a Reserve unit as a whole, it is not always possible for Reservists to receive formal classes in all the subjects they must know in order to advance in rank. It is therefore necessary for many Reservists to study training and maintenance manuals and sometimes participate in military correspondence courses.

Testing for promotion may involve written examinations as well as evaluation of job performance; in some instances, skill-level promotion qualifications may be determined by unit leaders only through observation of performance. Whatever system is used, many military leaders believe that members of the armed forces who study outside the classroom and on their own time, using personal study programs or correspondence courses, generally increase their overall proficiency and qualifications for advancement. Such off-duty study may indicate to a unit commander that an individual possesses the motivation needed to do well in the next higher rank. Personal study programs and correspondence courses completed at home must be planned in conjunction with family life and personal employment schedules.

The foregoing may seem to imply that Reserve service is a matter that constantly affects personal life—to the extent that such service is neither practical nor desirable. That is not the case, as shown by the successful service of millions who have served in the Reserve and Guard over the years.

The illustrations cited here are only for the purpose of advising young people that Reserve service is not simply a part-time job and something that can be entered into lightly. Hundreds of thousands of American men and women are serving as members of the Reserve forces at this time and finding the experience to be not a burden but a very positive influence in their lives. Many of them have found their service rewarding enough to remain in the Reserve forces for careers of twenty or more years. And many will tell you that any inconveniences relative to personal life are far outweighed by the benefits of Reserve service. Those benefits come in many forms and are accompanied by a bonus—the personal satisfaction that comes from serving as an important member of the U.S. Armed Forces.

The point we wish to convey is that life as a "citizen-soldier" is not always easy. It involves personal sacrifices and a large degree of personal responsibility; and it is a commitment that should be thoroughly discussed with family members and employers before being undertaken.

Part 2

THE RESERVE
COMPONENTS

Chapter III

The United States Army Reserve

The U.S. Army Reserve is the second largest of the seven Reserve components of America's armed forces (only the Army National Guard is larger). The modern Army Reserve evolved from the Medical Corps Reserve, which was created with just over 360 officers in 1908. Between World War I and World War II, twenty-six Army Reserve Divisions were established; all were mobilized for service in World War II.

Elements of the Army Reserve have continued to play major roles in America's international affairs since World War II. During the Korean War in the early 1950s, 244,000 Army Reservists were called to active duty. In 1961, when an international crisis developed concerning Berlin, the threat of conflict in Europe resulted in mobilization of 40,000 Army Reservists. During the Vietnam War just over 5,000 Army Reservists were mobilized, with 3,500 serving in Vietnam.

While some units of the Army Reserve are combat units, most provide combat support and combat service support. Combat units are trained and equipped for direct engagement with enemy forces in the event of conflict. Combat support units provide operational assistance to combat units and are often part of a theater, command, or task force formed for combat operations. Combat service support units provide essential services for combat and combat support units.

During the late 1960s a reorganization of the Army Reserve eliminated its combat divisions and placed most Army Reservists in combat support and combat service support units. In recent years the Army Reserve has consisted of more than 3,000 units. They are based and train at over 1,000 locations throughout the country, sometimes participating in exercises with elements of the active services both in the U.S. and overseas. The Army Reserve and Army National Guard account for about 50 percent of the total Army combat forces and approximately 80 percent of its logistics, service support, and wartime medical capabilities.

Beginning in the early 1980s, the Army Reserve began an intensive modernization program that led to a higher degree of combat readiness. Among elements receiving the most attention in the upgrading process were Army Reserve aviation units, which received significantly improved aircraft as replacements for aging equipment.

Today, almost everywhere the U.S. Army serves, Reservists can be found shoulder to shoulder with their active duty counterparts, performing the same missions or carrying out supporting roles that contribute substantially to combat readiness. More than 250 specialties are available to Army Reservists, ranging from law enforcement, data processing, military intelligence, equipment maintenance, and medical services to aviation-related fields and ballistic missile maintenance. Schools for military specialties are generally from eight to twelve weeks in duration and are usually completed during advanced individual training immediately after basic training. Basic training and advanced individual training may be split over two summers, a procedure that is sometimes helpful for high school graduates who are about to enter college during a fall semester.

Overseas deployment training helps prepare members of the Army Reserve for mobilization and increases the likelihood of a smooth transition from peacetime service to augmentation of the active force in wartime or other emergencies. Several thousand Army Reservists travel to overseas training locations each year with their own unit or as part of selected detachments or teams. The personnel participating in overseas training in a given year are usually not the same ones who took part in such programs over the previous few years; this permits the eventual travel to overseas training sites for larger numbers of Reservists. An entire Reserve unit might travel to Europe, South Korea, the Middle East, Central America, Japan, or another overseas location; or one or more members of a unit might be assigned to join soldiers from other Reserve units as part of command and control cells in an overseas special training program or field exercise with elements of the regular Army.

Following are representative Army Reserve drill, special training, and annual training duty activities that have taken place in the U.S. or overseas in recent years (for purposes of illustration, they are presented as a composite and in the present tense):

- Army Reserve pathfinder units travel to Europe for annual training duty and spend two weeks participating in a major North Atlantic Treaty Organization exercise with regular U.S. Army and allied forces. The pathfinders parachute into landing zones and help prepare the way for large numbers of personnel who will be transported into the area by helicopters.
- Members of Army Reserve civil affairs units travel to Central America to support elements of the regular forces and work with individual citizens and entire communities in projects such as road-building and medical assistance programs. Meanwhile, transportation and engineer units help repair old road networks and build new ones. Army Reservists with skills in supply and communications also support the operations.
- Lawyers who are Reserve officers and members of Reserve Judge Advocate General detachments report to major commands to support legal units of the regular Army. The Reserve attorneys are supported by enlisted Reservists who have been trained as legal specialists and, in some instances, hold civilian jobs in the legal field.
- Reserve truck drivers transport ammunition, water, food, and equipment repair parts to field training sites where

Army National Guard training can be very challenging. Here, members of an infantry unit learn special techniques for entering and departing tactical areas.

major training exercises involving Reserve and regular forces are under way. After establishing a field storage and maintenance facility for their vehicles, the drivers transport soldiers over rough terrain in training operations that test driver skills and the ability of their passengers to fight in motorized tactical operations. The training is monitored and supervised by Reserve officers and enlisted personnel who conducted similar operations during combat operations in Vietnam.

- Army Reserve helicopters take off on a mission to provide ground units with reconnaissance information on aggressor movements during a training exercise. In the course of their flight, the pilots receive a radio call requesting that they divert to another location to transport an injured soldier to a medical facility. The pilot and crew quickly complete the medical evacuation and return to their original mission. During that same field exercise, Army Reservists direct and fire artillery against simulated enemy tanks more than ten miles away, destroying all their targets in a matter of minutes.

- Boarding transports of the Air National Guard, members of an Army Reserve unit begin a series of flights that ultimately takes them to Germany. There they join elements of the Army in ground operations designed to teach them how to defend positions against massed formations of enemy tanks. They are supported by simulated bombing and strafing missions carried out by U.S. and allied aircraft. During their two-week stay in West Germany, the Reservists are permitted periods of free time in which to visit historic sites and tourist attractions. Before departing for home, they participate in a major multinational exercise designed to test their combat skills against enemy armor.

- At a major U.S. Army command, members of an Army Reserve engineer battalion report for annual training duty and immediately begin working with soldiers of the regular force in preventive maintenance of heavy equipment.

They then move to field training sites and undertake engineer operations as part of a larger force that is making rapid movements against objectives spread over several miles of rough terrain. The Reserve engineers man bulldozers and other heavy equipment to clear obstacles and help set in place bridges over deep streams and ravines.

• Members of an Army Reserve transportation company travel to an Air Force base, where they work with active force personnel in maintenance of Army Blackhawk helicopters. Already schooled in Blackhawk maintenance, they keep their skill levels high while awaiting Blackhawks that will eventually be assigned to their unit. Cooperation between Reserve and active forces is beneficial to both and results in a higher level of readiness for all. Training at active force schools and working with members of the other services, Army Reserve maintenance personnel develop and improve their proficiency in using and caring for aircraft survivability equipment, radar warning receivers, infrared warning devices, exhaust suppression systems, and other equipment used to reduce the possibility of detection of aircraft by enemy forces.

• In one of the Rocky Mountain states, members of an Army Reserve unit arrive for roll call at their local training center on a Saturday morning and before the day is over have used ropes to lower themselves from helicopters into a remote mountain region. There they practice mountain warfare techniques, wilderness survival, and land navigation before being extracted from the field training site by helicopters and returned to their unit on Sunday afternoon. After cleaning their weapons and equipment, they receive a critique on their performance during the drill and then depart for home.

• At another training center, Reservists of a ground transportation unit spend their weekend learning driving and maintenance techniques for a new type of high-mobility vehicle that is being introduced into the Army Reserve inventory. Although none of the vehicles have arrived at

Army Reservists frequently train with units of the regular Army and participate with them in field operations in the U.S. and overseas.

the unit, personnel who have already completed several days of formal instruction on the vehicle at a U.S. Army school teach other members of the unit, using training aids. When the new vehicles arrive a few weeks later, the unit is quickly able to begin using them safely and effectively. Familiar with cold-weather operations as a result of winter training in their own state, they travel to Alaska for annual training duty, which includes an exercise with an Army infantry division and members of the Canadian forces. In the course of their stay, they spend days trekking through ice-covered mountains while carrying out simulated assaults against an aggressor force. Their training completed, they return home with the knowledge that they will be better able to perform in actual combat with the Alaska-based infantry unit to which they expect to be assigned in the event of mobilization.

- Members of an Army Reserve unit in the southwestern U.S. travel to an Army training site that covers several thousand square miles of California desert. There they work with regular Army units in a series of simulated operations calling for high-speed movement through the desert during both day and night. Operating on foot and with tanks and armored personnel carriers, they spend long hours moving from one objective to another while firing live ammunition and directing artillery fire against targets along the route of travel. While moving at night, some use night vision goggles and other devices that permit soldiers to see targets and obstacles in darkness. Others attach to their rifles a small black box that directs an eye-safe laser against personnel and other targets; it is equipped with a device that sounds an alarm when touched by the laser beam. The system permits soldiers to determine if they would have scored a hit had they been using live ammunition.

• After traveling to Germany for annual training duty with her unit, a soldier prepares press releases and news stories about other members of the unit as they carry out field training with Army and allied forces. She takes photographs of individual Reservists in the field, processes the film at base photo laboratories, and sends the pictures with her stories to a central point from which they are distributed to newspapers and radio and television stations in the vicinity of her unit back in the U.S. After graduation from college with a degree in journalism, she will be able to use samples of her work as a Reservist as well as school projects in a portfolio for presentation to potential employers.

The examples cited here represent only a few of the many kinds of experiences Army Reservists may have in the course of service as citizen-soldiers. The opportunities available in more than 200 specialties permit Reservists to develop skills that may not only serve them and their country well in conjunction with their military service but may also open new windows of opportunity in civilian careers. After talking with Army Reserve

Army Reserves regularly test their mobilization readiness and the military skills of Individual members.

recruiters, discussing military occupational specialties, and examining closely the types of Reserve units in their home areas, persons joining the Reserve have a number of options from which to choose.

Many young men and women enter a delayed entry program before graduation from high school and do not undergo any formal training until reporting for active duty following graduation. Others may spend from several months to several years in the civilian work force or as college students before joining the Reserve either directly or through a delayed entry program.

Another method of entering the Army Reserve is through its Alternate Training Program. High school juniors and seniors can earn income, receive military training that may also be useful in a civilian career, and receive money for college tuition while still in high school. A high school senior entering the Alternate Training Program begins to receive monthly pay up to nine months before departing for basic training; a junior can receive pay three months before beginning basic training. In the period before reporting for basic training, the participant begins to learn about the Army and Army Reserve through limited training that brings a monthly pay check of more than $80. While at basic training during the summer between the junior and senior year or after graduation, earnings are more than $600 each month.

Like the Reserve components of all the Armed Forces, the Army offers a variety of methods of entry into its Reserve and a number of special programs that can be of benefit to those enlisting. The methods of entry and the programs change from time to time; therefore, in discussions with recruiters, prospective Reservists should always ask for an explanation of all options available at the time.

A review of available options is especially important to young people who are planning to attend college and also are interested in Reserve service. During the course of a college education, an enlisted Army Reservist's service normally earns him or her more than $7,000, which can be applied to college costs or other expenses. Other service-related tuition assistance is also available, including more than $5,000 under the Montgomery G.I. Bill and a benefit called the Student Loan Repayment Program, which allows the Army to repay 15 percent of a qualifying student loan, or $500, whichever is greater. Army Reservists who are also in the Army Reserve Officer Training Corps (ROTC) program during college can earn pay for both Reserve service and ROTC participation. The regulations that apply in the use of such programs tend to vary from year to year and should be discussed in detail with recruiters prior to entering Reserve service and with unit administrative personnel during service.

While much has been said, so far, about the benefits Reserve service may bring to civilian pursuits, there are also times when a civilian career can help a Reservist in carrying out military service. It is not uncommon for men and women in highly technical civilian jobs to use their skills and training on the job with their Reserve unit. This may lead to better chances for promotion when competing for a limited number of openings or for one of a limited number of job assignments available within a unit. Army Reserve commanders often find that the variety of civilian skills among Reservists are valuable when undertaking new technical programs or introducing new equipment that has already been in use in private business.

The type of Reserve units in or near one's home area often influences the type of military specialties and formal training available to prospective Reservists. Specialty training and assignment of military specialties usually must relate to the type of unit or units within reasonable traveling distance of a Reservist's home. The high percentage of combat support and combat service support units in the Army Reserve requires large numbers of Reservists skilled in many types of equipment maintenance and repair. Recruiters can advise applicants of the types of units in or near their home and the specialties most needed by those units.

Instruction received during basic training and in service schools during initial active duty for training is used as a base in the development of each Reservist's usefulness to his or her unit. Through drill periods and annual training duty, Army Reservists are expected to continually improve upon that base, expand their capabilities, and generally refine their proficiency in military specialties.

This all leads to highly capable Army Reserve units that serve as full partners in the Total Force, able to be mobilized quickly and assigned critical tasks on short notice.

Chapter **IV**

The Army National Guard

With more than 450,000 personnel in over 2,600 communities throughout the United States, the Army National Guard is the largest of the seven U.S. Reserve components. Its mission is to provide trained units and individuals in support of the Army's active component wartime force.

Unlike the Army Reserve, which is entirely a federal force, the Army National Guard has both federal and state missions. In their state role, Army National Guard units are responsible to the governor of the state in which they are located; at the same time, they are a major element of the federal defense system and in a national emergency may be either mobilized for extended active service or called to duty for brief periods with other elements of the Department of Defense.

Army National Guard training is usually administered by the Adjutant General in each state or territory. The Adjutant Generals work closely with the active Army in developing training programs to assure that units will be able to perform effectively with active units immediately upon mobilization.

The Army National Guard celebrated its 350th anniversary in 1986 and is considered the oldest military force in America. The first units of what eventually came to be called the National Guard were formed in Massachusetts beginning in 1636. Since that time, members of the Army National Guard have participated in every war or other conflict from the Revolution to Vietnam; they have also served in support of operations relating to international crises in the Middle East and other parts of the world in the years since the end of the Vietnam War. Forty percent of the Allied Expeditionary Force that served in

Europe during World War I was composed of Army National Guardsmen. During World War II more than 300,000 members of the Guard served on active duty, and 183,000 were called to active duty during the Korean War. In the Vietnam War, many of the more than 12,000 Army National Guard members who served on active duty distinguished themselves in combat operations in Southeast Asia.

A large percentage of the Army's combat forces are in the Army National Guard. Nearly 40 percent of the total Army combat divisions; more than 60 percent of its separate brigades; 40 percent of its engineer battalions; about 50 percent of its infantry battalions; and major portions of its artillery, armor, and other combat units are within the Army National Guard. Certain types of the total Army combat units reside only in the Army National Guard.

Because of the importance of its combat units to the overall national defense, the Army National Guard is equipped with some of the most up-to-date battle equipment available, including modern tanks, infantry fighting vehicles, missile carriers, howitzers, aircraft, communications equipment, and computers designed for military field operations. In view of the Army National Guard's anticipated role in the event of mobilization, many items of newly developed equipment are distributed to the Guard at the same time they are received by the regular Army.

The Army National Guard maintains more than 3,000 armories, nearly 1,000 maintenance shops, and about 100 aviation support facilities throughout the country. Many are manned at all times by full-time support personnel, including members of the Army Reserve and National Guard on full-time duty, Department of Defense civilian employees, and active Army personnel who help assure that most of the time Guard members spend at drill periods is in training and operations rather than on upkeep of facilities and administration. More than 50,000 people are assigned to full-time support duties with the Army National Guard.

In addition to training at facilities in and near their home-

Members of the Guard and Reserve must be able to fight when under attack by forces using chemical warfare. Here, Virginia Army National Guardsmen use gas masks while operating weapons and equipment.

town, members of the Guard often attend annual training duty at active force training sites, which may be nearby or in distant locations, including overseas. In one recent year nearly 40,000 members of the Army National Guard participated in overseas training in forty countries. More than 5,000 from twenty-six states participated in a single major exercise that took them to Europe. In one summer, 10,000 members of the Army National Guard from around the country took part in a road-building operation the Amazon basin in South America. Weekend drills may include travel to and from distant locations in government-provided transportation; however, most weekend sessions are at or near the home training center.

Sometimes the two-week annual training duty is spent undergoing testing and evaluation in tactics and operational procedures to determine unit and individual combat readiness. Evaluations of the units are carried out by active duty soldiers, who measure Guard performance against active Army unit standards and capabilities.

In their state role, members of the Army National Guard often provide emergency services that benefit many of the citizens in their region. Almost every year, thousands of Guard personnel are called to service by the governor of the state in response to civil emergencies, usually natural disasters. In one recent year, 623 such call-ups involved nearly 30,000 members of the Army Guard. The emergencies are varied, but most calls to active service for the states come in the aftermath of tornadoes, floods, blizzards, and other acts of nature. Guard members may use heavy equipment to help clear highways and restore services or may even be employed to prevent looting when commercial or residential areas have been damaged severely or evacuated.

Another role undertaken by the Army National Guard in recent years has been in support of federal and state efforts to cut the flow of illegal drugs into this country and interdiction of distribution of such drugs as have been smuggled in. As part of their duties with their home state or in support of federal law enforcement operations, members of the Guard have assisted in the confiscation and destruction of millions of dollars worth of illegal substances.

The following activities and events actually took place over a short period of time within the recent past; they are presented as a composite and in the present tense to help illustrate the many activities that may be undertaken, and the types of skills needed, among units of the Army National Guard at any given time:

- In California members of Army National Guard units join forces with elements of the Air Guard to help airlift more than 2,000 flood victims from their homes and businesses after major storms devastate large areas near San Francisco. Guard personnel are credited with saving thirty-three lives in the emergency.
- A battalion from an air defense artillery unit in New Mexico becomes the first unit in the total Army to receive and become qualified to employ in operations a new mis-

sile system called the Roland. The weapon is used to protect troops on the ground and in vehicles from low-altitude attacks by enemy aircraft.

- As part of their annual training duty, an armor unit of the Nevada Army National Guard drives 180 vehicles, including forty-three tanks, across the Mojave Desert to a major Army training and testing center in California and then returns home over the same route; temperatures during the trips sometimes reach 110 degrees. Several months later the same unit undergoes annual training in subfreezing weather at a base in Minnesota near the Canadian border.

- During annual training duty that took his unit to Panama, an Army National Guardsman uses his free time to help a Panamanian church congregation repair their chapel. Wood for the project came from trees cleared in a road-building operation undertaken by 10,000 members of the Guard over a period of several months. During the same operation, a medical unit from Alabama provides outpatient services for dozens of Panamanian citizens.

- Elsewhere in Latin America, an Army National Guard unit from Louisiana arrives for annual training duty that will include bridge construction in remote areas. In addition to military engineering equipment, Guard personnel bring to the region several tons of toys, clothing, and other refugee relief items donated by private groups in the U.S.

- At an Army base in Maryland, a group of Nurse Corps officers of the Army National Guard report for an eight-day combat nursing course. Some of them have traveled from as far away as Alaska. Included in the course are classes in advanced trauma life support, treatment of victims of chemical warfare, field sanitation, survival skills, and escape and evasion techniques. When instruction is completed, the twenty graduating nurses return to their units, where they instruct other members of the Guard in field medical procedures.

- In a small town in West Germany, several Army National

Guard representatives arrive to participate in an international biathlon, a competition that combines cross-country skiing and target shooting. The U.S. citizen-soldier athletes had earlier competed in a similar competition in Italy and were among more than 160 men and women of the National Guard from thirty-two states who had qualified for the European events during championship events in Vermont.

* Army National Guard attack helicopters from mid-Atlantic states arrive at a firing range in Virginia on a Saturday for a weekend of gunnery practice against several types of targets. Pilots and maintenance crews prepare their aircraft for the type of missions they would be called upon to perform in combat before the helicopters take to the air for their missions in a steady rain. Firing rockets, machine guns, and grenades, the helicopters assault their targets for several hours before the pilots return to a field landing site. There crews perform maintenance on weapons and communications equipment before the unit settles into its tent camp for the night. Training is completed on Sunday morning, and units are back at their home training centers by Sunday evening.

* In Florida, an Army National Guard artillery unit from Puerto Rico arrives at a large base for annual training duty that will include long-range gunnery practice. The unit and its weapons fly to Florida in Air National Guard transports. Shortly after arrival, its artillery pieces are engaged against targets several miles away. Part of the training program includes the rapid movement of field artillery pieces to new locations, using trucks to tow them and helicopters to lift them. The unit's communications specialists maintain continuous radio contact with other units while the movements are carried out.

* In the Black Hills of South Dakota, a Guard engineer unit conducts its annual training at an abandoned uranium mine. Using bulldozers and other heavy equipment, the soldiers fill in old mines and perform other field operations

that help improve safety conditions at the site. While conducting the work, they carry out security training that prepares them for engineer operations in combat situations.

- Soldiers of the Oregon National Guard travel to southern California for annual training duty. In San Diego they board U.S. Navy ships for a short cruise along the coast before conducting an amphibious landing at a Marine Corps base. The exercise includes ship-to-shore transport of their vehicles and other equipment under simulated combat conditions. Once ashore, the soldiers conduct combat training operations against objectives designed to test their teamwork and knowledge of small unit tactics.

- In Nebraska a helicopter from an Army National Guard air ambulance company is prepared for flight. The pilot, copilot, crew chief, and flight medic are all women. Their mission takes them to a point several miles away, where they pick up another member of the Guard who has a simulated injury and return him to a field medical facility. In a wartime situation or civil emergency, the team aboard the helicopter might be called upon to operate for extended periods of time under extremely difficult conditions; frequent practice flights and occasional missions involving the evacuation of persons suffering from actual illnesses or injuries during weekend drills and annual training duty prepare them for such an eventuality.

- One of the country's top amateur wrestlers, who is also a college student in Hawaii, takes time from training and studies to perform weekend training as a fire direction chief for an Army National Guard artillery unit. He works with other members of the unit in computing figures needed to assure that fire from artillery pieces lands on targets designated by observers on the ground or in airplanes several miles away. His college studies in mechanical engineering are being paid for with several thousand dollars that he saved under the Veterans Educational Assistance Program while in the active Army and additional assistance earned through service in the Guard.

- Three members of the Wyoming Army National Guard and two members of the state's Air National Guard—all of whom work for the same chemical company in civilian life—are honored at a luncheon ceremony by their employer. Attending the function is the Wyoming Adjutant General, who represents the governor. He joins an executive of the chemical company in recognizing the five Guard members for their service in national defense.
- Dozens of members of the Army National Guard from around the nation gather with representatives of the Air Guard at a rifle range near Phoenix, Arizona. There they take part in a week-long rifle competition in which they fire their service rifles at targets over distances of up to 600 yards. The top shooters in the event are assigned to the All Guard Rifle Squad, which then competes against members of other Reserve and active force components during national shooting matches in Ohio.
- Dust trails across the floor of a canyon in the Mojave Desert in California signal the approach of tanks and other combat vehicles operated by South Carolina Army National Guard troops. Members of an armored battalion, they have traveled across the United States to the Army National Training Center, where they participate in simulated warfare using tanks and other equipment provided by the training facility. Because of the size of the training area, they are able to employ all of their own weapons and call in live supporting fire from artillery and aircraft as they move quickly over extended distances practicing gunnery, tactical maneuvering, air defense, chemical warfare defense, and command and control operations. Members of the South Carolina unit include drivers of tanks and other armored vehicles as well as Guardsmen trained in heavy equipment repair, communications, supply, and several other specialties needed for fielding an effective armored unit.
- British paratroopers of a parachute regiment arrive in Florida to spend two weeks training with the Florida

Army National Guard. At the same time, an infantry company from the Florida Guard travels to Wales for annual training duty with the parachute regiment. The units involved in the exchange program conduct their training over terrain substantially different from what they have been used to and learn to operate weapons and equipment of their host units.

• During weekend training at their local Maryland Army National Guard training center, personnel of a Guard supply and transportation unit learn of a railroad accident nearby. Men and women of the Guard quickly divert from their normal training operations to participate in the medical evacuation of many of the nearly 200 people injured in the wreck. As three Army Guard helicopters lift the patients to nearby hospitals, an off-duty Air National Guard nurse who learned of the accident applies lifesaving techniques on some of the severely injured victims as they are transported from the disaster area.

Every drill weekend for members of the Army National Guard—and for all the Reserve forces—is planned well in advance by unit leaders assisted by full-time support personnel. Training plans are developed to meet specific objectives designed to prepare units for the jobs they will be assigned in the event of war. Often drills are focused on unit training in which all members participate as a team to perfect the skills needed to accomplish mission-related tasks. In some cases, however, drill periods are dedicated to individual training in which each member of the unit works on improving his or her specialty or improving proficiency in general military subjects. This may mean work in a classroom at the training center or operations at a nearby field training site. Whatever the location, training is supervised by experienced officers and senior enlisted personnel and may include formal or informal testing to determine skill levels.

In most instances, members of the Guard are advised well in advance if their drill weekends will involve remaining overnight at the local training center or at a field location. Usually when training is conducted at the unit's armory or other nearby facility, Guard members go home on Saturday evening and return to the training site on Sunday morning.

Members of the Army National Guard have the opportunity to improve their skills and proficiency during nonduty periods throughout the month. Those who do so through correspondence courses or other means generally find that such self-guided training not only improves their performance of duty but often leads to faster promotions to positions of greater responsibility and leadership in their unit.

While the weekend drills and annual training duty prepare Army National Guard units for general mobilization, that team training also prepares units and individuals for many of the tasks that they are called upon to perform for their home state in emergency situations. Their dual role—which makes them responsible to federal and state authorities—helps build among members of the Army National Guard a unique bond that extends into their civilian occupations and careers. Few forms of service to community and country are more personally rewarding.

Chapter V

The United States Air Force Reserve

Origins of the Air Force Reserve date to the earliest days of aviation, when military personnel began to look into the possibility of using airplanes for defense purposes. It was not until 1916, however, that the National Defense Act of that year authorized assignment of nearly 300 officers and 2,000 enlisted men to serve in an aviation section of the Signal Reserve Corps. The first Reserve squadron was formed in New York State and later was mobilized for World War I service in France. More aviation Reservists were deployed to Europe, and hundreds eventually served as pilots, members of air crews, and in ground support roles during the war. Pilots were trained in civilian aviation schools and received advanced lessons in flying and aerial tactics from U.S. Army flying schools.

During World War II, Reserve pilots served with the Army Air Corps. The Army Air Forces Reserve became the Air Force Reserve in the late 1940s, when the Air Force became a separate component of the U.S. Armed Forces. Many veterans of World War II were among the Air Force Reservists who were called to active duty or volunteered for service in the early 1950s during the Korean War, when many Reserve units were placed in an active duty status.

Between the Korean War and the war in Vietnam, the Air Force Reserve underwent many changes as new and sophisticated types of aircraft and weapons systems entered service. At the same time, the importance of the Reserve continued to grow as more and more operational missions were carried out by Reserve units or Reservists working with active force units. During an international crisis between the Soviet Union and the United States with its European allies in the early 1960s, several thousand Air Force Reservists served on active duty and participated in operations that helped end the tension without conflict.

A short time later, in 1962, nearly 15,000 Air Force Reservists were among members of the Reserve Forces who served on active duty during a period of near-war. The Soviet Union had armed Cuban forces with missiles that could have been fired at the United States. A show of force by the United States—including activation of Reserve units—helped convince the Soviet Union that it should dismantle missile sites in Cuba. Later in that same decade, another crisis in the Caribbean—this time, a revolution in the Dominican Republic—led to the use of Reserve air crews to fly food, supplies, and equipment in support of U.S. operations there.

During the early days of the Vietnam War, many individual Air Force Reservists participated in flights to and from the combat zone; later, entire Reserve units were called to active duty either to serve in Vietnam or to temporarily cover commitments for active force units that were deployed to Southeast Asia.

In periods of international tension in the eastern Mediterranean in the 1970s and 1980s and the Persian Gulf in the late 1980s, Air Force Reservists again demonstrated both their value and readiness as they participated in support missions. Some of those missions included flights to the operational areas.

Ready and Responsive

The Air Force Reserve frequently responds to situations as rapidly and effectively as elements of the active Air Force. In addition to their role in support of U.S. objectives in the Middle East, other situations in which Air Force Reservists have played key roles in the 1980s further illustrate the importance of their military duties.

In one recent 48-month period they assisted earthquake victims in Ecuador and Mexico; used aircraft to spray disease-bearing mosquitoes in Puerto Rico and grasshoppers in a major plague in the western U.S.; flew relief missions for drought-stricken farmers in the Midwestern and Western U.S.; helped the victims of volcanic eruptions in Colombia; saved people stranded in blizzards; evacuated victims of a fire in Puerto Rico to hospitals in the continental U.S.; took part in aerial fire-fighting missions over burning parklands; flew refueling missions in support of America's nuclear deterrent forces and European tanker task force; and carried out thousands of other routine transport missions in support of Reserve and active force missions of all the Armed Forces.

Many of those missions were accomplished during "drill weekends," but others were conducted outside of formal unit drill periods by Air Force Reserve crews working on special Reserve-flown missions or in conjunction with regular Air Force operations.

Those achievements demonstrate both the capabilities and the responsiveness of the Air Force Reserve. They help explain why Air Force leaders emphasize that their Reserve units are not manned by "weekend warriors"—a term sometimes applied to Reservists—but by true citizen-soldiers who share the full-time responsibilities of national defense. Those accomplishments also show that service as an Air Force Reservist is by no means restricted to weekend training at a local airport or military air base.

To fulfill their duties, Air Force Reservists not only use equipment transferred to them from the active forces but are also provided with brand-new aircraft and other equipment directly from the country's defense suppliers. Operating aircraft comparable to those of the active forces and training under the same standards assures proficiency among members of the Reserve and helps create confidence among active Air Force personnel that, in the event of mobilization, Reservists

Among a variety of planes kept in a high state of readiness and flown by Air National Guard personnel are A-10 attack aircraft.

will make the transition to full-time service smoothly and quickly.

Unit Training

The many types of aircraft flown by Air Force Reserve pilots and the general operations of a large military force create a wide range of specialties available to Air Force Reservists. Administrative requirements for personnel, maintenance, and supply create a need for substantial numbers of people qualified in office management, bookkeeping, financial management, inventory control, maintenance management, and computer programming. All of those specialties and many others are in direct support of Reserve men and women who maintain Air Force Reserve aircraft and fly them as pilots and crew members.

In many instances, Air Force Reservists routinely carry out their jobs one weekend a month at a local Air Force Reserve training facility—often at or near a civilian airport or aboard a military air base. The nature of air operations and training are such, however, that it is not uncommon for the Reservists—particularly pilots and air crews—to fulfill their drill requirements during the week while flying support or operational missions with active duty pilots and crews, and sometimes in aircraft of the regular Air Force.

Individual Mobilization Augmentees

The Air Force Reserve Individual Mobilization Augmentee (IMA) Program is designed to help the Air Force retain a strong base of trained personnel both for peacetime use and to help strengthen fighting capabilities in the event of mobilization. The program keeps former active Air Force members involved in operations with active duty personnel; in the event of mobilization, program participants may become full-time members of the Air Force team.

Instead of being assigned to a hometown Reserve unit, IMA

members work with active force units. Sometimes a Reservist is assigned to an active force unit near his or her home; but assignment may be with a unit across the country. In the latter case the Reservist may participate in monthly training with a Reserve or active force unit close to home. Annual training duty, however, will be with the active duty unit to which he or she is assigned.

An IMA member generally has more flexibility in training than other Reservists because training periods can be tailored to fit his or her civilian work schedule and personal commitments such as family responsibilities or college classes. The IMA earns Reserve pay and allowances, points toward retirement, and training and experience that are often valuable in civilian pursuits. Additionally, an IMA member may earn additional pay and retirement points by serving additional training periods each month or participating in active duty over a period of days, weeks, or months.

The IMA Program is well worth considering by persons interested in Air Force Reserve service whose long-term personal goals and obligations permit them to serve on active duty for a few years before beginning Reserve service. Upon return to civilian life they continue to pursue Air Force careers on a part-time basis in fields such as legal services, medical services, civil engineering, research and development, security, and many others.

Drill Periods

The drill activities in the Air Force Reserve vary widely depending on the type of unit and the occupational specialties within the unit. If a Reservist is not a pilot or other crew member of an aircraft, drill periods may be spent maintaining or servicing aircraft, maintaining and servicing other unit equipment, or participating in the administration and logistical support activities that are required of all active and Reserve units.

Dozens of skills are required in the Air Force Reserve relating to both aviation and nonaviation functions. During any drill period a flying unit may need Reservists skilled not only in flying but also in electronics, telephone repair, jet engine mechanics, plumbing, carpentry, motor vehicle operations and repair, firefighting, bulk fuel storage and transport, first aid, and many other specialties.

Other nonflying units need many of the already mentioned skills as well as others in a wide range of technical and non-technical areas. Regardless of the skills employed by any Reserve unit, however, the overall objective remains the same: to assure that the Air Force Reserve, in total, is continually

Air Force Reserve and Air National Guard weapons technicians must be prepared to handle large amounts of high explosives quickly and safely.

able to carry out a number of peacetime operational responsibilities and stand ready to bolster the active forces with well-trained, well-equipped personnel in the event of war or other circumstances calling for mobilization.

The young Air Force Reservist fresh from basic and specialty training may report from initial active duty to a tactical aircraft squadron for his or her first weekend drill and begin serving in a maintenance position beside a veteran of many years of Reserve service. Or the first weekend drill may be with a flying crew aboard a transport aircraft participating in the emergency airlift of supplies to flood victims. Hundreds of skills in jobs in the air and on the ground are required to keep the Air Force Reserve flying.

Training and Operations

Following are actual training and operational activities carried out by Air Force Reservists at various locations and times in recent years; for the purpose of illustrating how far-ranging and diverse Air Force Reserve activities may be, they are presented in the present tense and as a composite:

- In Pittsburgh, Pennsylvania, a Master Sergeant with more than forty years of active and Reserve service steps down from a C-130 aircraft after his final mission as a flight engineer before retiring from the Reserve. He has logged more than 12,000 hours of flying time with his local unit as both a Reservist and a civilian technician. At about the same time, in San Antonio, Texas, another Reservist becomes the first woman, regular or Reserve, to serve as a flight engineer/flight examiner for C-5 aircraft of the Military Airlift Command. During service in the active Air Force and as a Reservist, she has attained more than 2,300 hours of flight time and eight years of experience in the giant transports.
- At McGuire Air Force Base in New Jersey, members of an Air Force Reserve crew of a military airlift squadron

from points as far away as Illinois and North Carolina check out their aircraft and prepare for overseas flight before departing with passengers and cargo for air bases in the Azores and West Germany. They will return to their home base by way of Washington, D.C., where patients medically evacuated from hospitals in Europe will be transferred from aircraft to waiting ground transportation bound for hospitals in the U.S. All the Reserve aircraft crew members are part of the Reserve Associate Program, in which Reservists share aircraft with active duty units and often fly similar missions. The Reservists come from varying civilian backgrounds: One of the pilots for the flight is also a pilot for a major civilian airline; a flight examiner and loadmaster is a policeman from New York City; one of three Reservists serving as nurses for the patients is an emergency medical technician and nurse for a medical center rescue helicopter in Savannah, Georgia —another is a vocational school teacher.

- At another Air Force Reserve unit, four Reservists complete building a piece of equipment that will be used to help train pilots and crews who are about to receive a different type of aircraft from those they have been flying. The Reservists worked on the project for two months and in the process saved the Air Force thousands of dollars by using spare parts and modeling the equipment after another training device of similar design.

- In Texas, an Air Force Reserve crew, flying its unit's own C-5 transport aircraft, departs on a weekend mission that will include moving a single load of supplies and equipment weighing more than 100,000 pounds a distance of more than 1,200 miles. At another Reserve unit, in Utah, pilots and support personnel prepare for the Air Force Tactical Gunnery Competition in which the service's "Top Gun," from among all of its regular and Reserve pilots, is determined. A pilot from the Utah unit won that competition in 1987, pilots from the same wing won second and fifth place, and a Reserve team from a unit in Louisiana took first place in a related maintenance competition. Air Force Reserve teams have also won the first-place trophy for refueling operations in Strategic Air Command bombing and navigation competitions, taken first place in search and rescue competitions sponsored by the U.S. Air Force and Canadian Forces, and won top honors in the C-141 and C-130 aircraft categories during the Military Airlift Command's worldwide Airlift Rodeo competition.

• When U.S. Army medical personnel deploy to Honduras to work at a base there, they are joined by an Air Force Reservist who is chief nurse with a tactical clinic at an Air Force base in Texas. Air Force Reserve crews supported the airlift mission that took the medical specialists to Central America. At a more distant location—Osan, Korea— an Air Force Reserve aerial port squadron from

Airlift units of the Air Force Reserve often move U.S. Army, Army Reserve, and Army National Guard personnel and equipment to distant locations.

San Francisco arrives for annual training duty; they take on a number of duties, including aerial port administration, cargo processing and load planning, and air terminal operations.

- An entirely different type of mission is undertaken by Air Force Reservists from Ohio, who serve as crews and technicians on aerial spraying flights over Idaho to stop an infestation of grasshoppers covering thousands of acres of farmland. Spraying undertaken by the unit was similar to the type of operation it might be called upon to carry out against mosquitoes or other disease-bearing insects during combat operations. The unit's mission is successful, and it earns a commendation from the Governor of Idaho.

- At the Air Force Office of Scientific Research in Washington, D.C., a research scientist who is also an Individual Mobilization Augmentee in the Air Force Reserve, conducts experiments with molten salts during drill periods. He is one of nearly four dozen Reservists assigned to the unit, nearly half of whom hold doctorates in chemistry, electronics, physics, computer sciences, or other highly specialized disciplines.

- A civilian aircraft with only the pilot aboard strays off course and heads out to sea off Florida; the pilot does not respond to radio calls, and other pilots observing him at close range determine that he is unconscious. When the plane runs out of fuel and drops into the sea, two Air Force Reserve search and rescue parachutists jump into the water from a following aircraft and help save the pilot, who had regained consciousness and escaped his sinking plane.

- In Alaska, Reserve pilots and crews work alongside active duty personnel on a major Reserve-sponsored exercise in which large numbers of U.S. Army troops and large loads of equipment and supplies are dropped by parachute into rugged snow-covered mountains. The transports fly close to the ground to evade active Air Force planes that simulate attacking Soviet aircraft. During the same exercise, some of the Reserve planes land on short dirt runways to practice combat off-loading of cargo at high speed.

The foregoing Reserve activities are actual events that occurred in recent years, but many such operational and training activities could be taking place at almost any time throughout the year at Air Force Reserve training sites across America or during exercises in foreign locations. The intensive requirements placed on individual Air Force Reservists help ensure that the national defense is in a high state of readiness, but those demands also result in experience and experiences that are personally rewarding to the thousands of men and women who commit to such demanding service.

The entire process has been aptly described by one Air Force Reserve general officer: "Our bottom line is that skilled people plus modern equipment equal combat readiness."

Chapter VI

The Air National Guard

The mission of the Air National Guard is to provide trained units and qualified personnel for active federal service in time of national emergency if additional forces are needed. This means that members of the Air National Guard may be called to active federal duty not only in the event of general war but also when the country is under threat of war or facing other types of emergencies.

Like the Army National Guard, Air National Guard units, when in a nonmobilized status, are commanded by the state and territorial governors. In peacetime Air National Guard units are assigned to the Air Force commands with which they will operate in the event of mobilization and must be immediately deployable in support of Air Force operational requirements.

The National Guard first became involved in adapting aircraft for military use in 1911, when members of the New York National Guard flew an early plane. Later, Guard elements in California and Missouri started flying units, and in 1915 a New York aviation unit gained federal recognition as the National Guard's first official air unit. That unit was among elements of the Guard that were called to active duty in 1916 to patrol the Mexican border following incidents of concern to the federal government.

The Air National Guard was officially established as a separate component in 1947 and since 1950 has participated in every national emergency in which Reserve forces have been used. Four of the thirty-seven jet pilots who became aces during the Korean War (each having destroyed at least five enemy aircraft) were members of the Air National Guard. Members of the Air National Guard were mobilized during the Berlin crisis of the early 1960s, more than 10,000 were activated during the Vietnam War, and more than 2,000 eventually served in Southeast Asia.

Air National Guard Operations

Units of the Air National Guard are generally at the disposal of their home state for use in emergencies but must be prepared for immediate deployment in support of the needs of the Department of Defense. In recent years Air National Guard personnel have constituted about 30 percent of the total Air Force; included in their equipment are about 1,800 aircraft flown by more than 90 flying squadrons.

Every day of the year, Air Guard fighter interceptor aircraft are airborne over the United States, guarding the borders against incursions by aircraft of foreign governments, including possible attack forces. It is not uncommon on those missions to encounter Soviet bombers near U.S. air space. When such meetings occur, the Guard pilots often follow the movements of the Soviet planes until they are no longer in threatening positions. Air National Guard fighter interceptors fly nearly 90 percent of the total Air Force fighter interceptor missions, about half of its tactical reconnaissance flights, and large portions of its tactical transport and tactical fighter missions.

Air National Guard pilots and crews have some of the highest averages of flying time of all U.S. military pilots. Because many of them have extensive active duty before entering the Guard and because of the numerous missions they carry out during the year, pilots in tactical and strategic airlift units average more than 2,800 hours flying time. Another reason for such high levels of experience is aggressive training programs in which entire units deploy to worldwide locations every three years; partial units or individual air crews make such deployments even more often. In one recent year more than 39,000 Air and Army National Guard troops participated in overseas training in forty-four countries. In many instances, the Air National Guard supported the Army National Guard in those deployments, which included sixty-nine training exercises with other U.S. and allied forces. Members of the Air National Guard were among more than 9,000 members of the Guard from forty-three states and territories trained in Central America during that year.

The Air National Guard has about 1,300 units, many of which operate from its more than 150 installations. They are located in every state, the District of Columbia, Puerto Rico, the Virgin Islands, and Guam, and most are supported by more than 100 communications-electronics units operated by the Air National Guard. The Guard also has a number of engineering and service units, which not only provide internal services but also deploy to locations throughout the United States and around the world in support of other American forces and interests. They provide base services, engineering and fire protection, disaster relief, and explosive ordnance disposal.

Not all Air National Guard units are directly involved with flying operations; however, the flying units are equipped with some of the latest aircraft available to U.S. forces, and the equipment on the planes is often the most up-to-date available in high technology. This ranges from communications equipment to systems that help pilots carry out tactical missions at night and in all weather conditions.

The missions of flying units are wide-ranging. Tactical fighter aircraft are used to seek and engage enemy aircraft; tactical transports ferry men and equipment in support of ground, air, and sea operations; strategic transport aircraft support the strategic forces and include tankers that refuel long-range bombers; tactical reconnaissance aircraft seek information on enemy strengths and locations; attack aircraft engage enemy targets on the ground and at sea; helicopters are used for observation, transportation of personnel and equipment, and search and rescue missions. A number of aircraft are used for special training and support missions. In all, the Air National Guard operates more than 1,500 aircraft.

Demand is continuous for highly qualified men and women to fly, maintain, and repair the Air National Guard's aviation fleet and for thousands of others to carry out operational and training duties in specialties ranging from the technical to administrative.

Unit Training and Operations

To meet its responsibilities in shouldering a major portion of the aviation responsibilities of the U.S. Armed Forces, the Air National Guard conducts many types of training in many locations. Much of its activity is directed not just at training but also at carrying out operational missions, most of which relate to national defense. The following composite of events, which actually occurred over a period of several months in the recent past, illustrates the types of training and operations carried out during weekend drills, annual training duty, and other periods of service:

- Members of a tactical airlift group of the North Carolina Air National Guard return to their home unit bearing trophies that represent first place as the best tactical airlift group in the Free World. Competing against units of the Air Force, Air Force Reserve, Marine Corps, and allied airlift teams from around the world, the North Carolina unit compiled the most points, using a twenty-seven-year-old aircraft so well maintained that it outperformed many newer models. Crews took the plane through a number of lift missions, transporting containers, heavy equipment, and personnel. Phases of the competition involved the dropping of cargo by parachute, navigation, flight safety, and short airfield landings.
- A tactical fighter wing from the District of Columbia flies to Keflavik, Iceland, and two weeks of missions over open ocean. For many units annual training duty is conducted during the summer, but in this instance it is April and still very cold over the North Atlantic as the unit trains and

operates with Air Forces Iceland and other elements of North Atlantic Treaty Organization (NATO) forces stationed in Iceland. Flights include aerial combat training against U.S. Air Force fighters and searches for possible Soviet bombers and other aircraft that often approach Iceland on long-range patrols. Other training includes participation in an exercise that takes aircraft and crews to the Royal Air Force base at Lossiemouth, Scotland.

- A few weeks after the return of that unit to the District of Columbia, more than 600 Air National Guardsmen from another location depart for exercises that involve flights to Spain, Italy, England, and Germany. A transport unit, it moves large amounts of equipment and personnel, including several military patients, for U.S. and allied forces participating in exercises in southern Europe. Ground crews work in three overlapping shifts to enable the unit to fly nearly 130,000 miles in more than 500 flying hours while lifting 430 tons of cargo and supporting drops by nearly 2,000 paratroopers.

- A pilot with an air refueling squadron in the Kansas Air National Guard reports for monthly training and performs work similar to that done in his civilian career. A test pilot with one of the nation's largest aircraft manufacturers, he has logged more than 8,500 hours of flight time in 80 types of aircraft. His civilian occupation is a direct result of the flight training that he received in the Air Force and continued in the Air National Guard.

- In South Dakota, a farmer and agricultural pilot from Minnesota adjusts his flight helmet and climbs into the cockpit of an attack jet. A veteran of more than 300 missions over Vietnam and several months of ground duty in that country controlling the air strikes of U.S. aircraft, he is now a member of the South Dakota Air National Guard and is preparing to depart on a training mission. It will take him to the skies over Kansas where he and another pilot will perform simulated attacks against targets designated by a U.S. Army infantry division conducting field training.

Pilots and ground crews of the South Dakota Guard have helped bring home some of the Air Force's top honors for unit skills and proficiency; the mission to Kansas will help sharpen those skills. In addition to a number of other Midwestern farmers, members of the unit who report for drills and annual training duty include businessmen, farmers, airline pilots, realtors, and stockbrokers. Several are veterans of active duty with the Air Force, Navy, and Marine Corps; but many entered the Air National Guard directly and carry the same workloads as veterans of extended active service.

- Another Air National Guard unit deploys to Panama with five aircraft and fifty-four people. For two weeks they fly training missions in support of an Army infantry brigade that guards the canal. On an earlier annual training duty trip to that country the same unit was directed to extend its stay when civil war erupted in another Latin American country. Although the unit was not called on to act in the crisis, it stood ready to do so and thus was part of a U.S. signal of concern about one of its neighbors in the Western Hemisphere.

- Members of a New York Air National Guard rescue and recovery unit routinely conduct lifesaving operations in the waters off Long Island. Helicopter crew members have used hoisting lines, and parachutists from the unit have made many jumps into the Atlantic to save injured sailors and fishermen. Included in weekend training for some of the pararescue personnel have been free-fall jumps from 13,000 feet. When their peacetime training sessions are diverted to become lifesaving missions, unit personnel perform many of the search and rescue techniques they would employ in combat situations. Upon mobilization, their job would be to help rescue combat pilots whose aircraft had gone down over sea or land.

- At an Air National Guard base in the Midwest, an urgent call is received for help in delivering a donor heart for an infant dying of heart disease. The governor of the state has approved use of an aircraft that had been on alert as part of the defense of North America. The Guard pilot takes off for California, where the transplant operation is successfully completed at Stanford University Medical School a few hours later.

- A detachment of Air National Guard personnel from units in upstate New York carry out a training exercise designed to prepare them for response to blizzard conditions striking a major metropolitan area. They are trained in assisting individual citizens, schools, and businesses should a snowstorm leave several feet of snow, downing power lines, disrupting road and rail traffic, and creating life-threatening situations. Among the more than sixty personnel participating in the exercise, several had been involved in real snow emergency rescue operations in the region in previous winters.

- For operations in snow of even greater depths, another Air National Guard unit equips its transport planes with ski-like landing gear. The unit departs from the East Coast and flies to Antarctica in support of scientists of the National Oceanographic and Atmospheric Administration while the U.S. Navy unit that usually supports the scientists is performing maintenance on its aircraft. Air National Guard crews participating in the operation are familiar with operating and maintaining aircraft in severe cold; for several years they have been conducting air resupply missions as far north as Greenland.

- Another Air National Guard unit—a tactical fighter group from Texas—spends several drill periods preparing its airplanes and support equipment for overseas flights. Then for annual training duty the members deploy nearly 4,000 miles to Turkey to support U.S. and allied forces training in the eastern Mediterranean. While the unit and a number of its full-time support members are there, maintenance crews work on aircraft between flights, an administrative staff manages unit records, and supply personnel distribute parts and other supplies as they are called for. Air National Guard technicians who have been trained at Air Force communications and electronics schools quickly repair or replace equipment as their unit's aircraft carry out intensive tactical training.

• Journeying to an even more remote location, members of an Air National Guard tactical airlift group from a mid-Atlantic state join Air National Guard units from eleven other states in deploying to Ecuador. There they provide transport assistance to Army National Guard and Reserve engineers who are building a road in the jungle. While in South America the unit is called on to provide transportation for a delegation of visiting members of the U.S. Congress and senior Air Force officers.

The foregoing examples of actual Air National Guard training and operations missions provide just a glimpse of the many jobs performed by members of that Reserve component. To conduct such missions, to complete them on time and often under difficult conditions, the Guard relies on the skills of individual members. There are few better examples of the positive results that can be achieved through teamwork. Senior officers of the Air National Guard stress that fact—that individuals and units must comprise a single team prepared for instant response in the event of mobilization.

Many of the examples used have been flying units that regularly carry out movements to distant locations. However, members of many base, communications support, and other types of units routinely carry out monthly drills at their hometown location and travel to distant points only during annual training duty, for special training, or to attend military schools.

As noted earlier, members of the Reserve and National Guard are usually assigned to units in or near their hometown. The Air National Guard is among the Reserve components that have numbers of members who travel long distances to attend monthly training. They are usually pilots and other aircraft crew members who have served beyond their obligated service and intend to remain in the Guard to earn enough service points for retirement benefits. There may be no openings available in units in their home area, or they may be qualified to operate aircraft or equipment that is not used by the nearby Air National Guard units.

The training that members of the Air National Guard receive during initial active duty, the specialty schools they attend, and the on-the-job training they receive with units near their home and during annual training duty are all designed with readiness in mind. Professional military education is an essential part of the programs used to develop technical proficiency and ability to work under extremely trying conditions—the type of conditions frequently encountered in combat situations. The Air National Guard has established realistic training, both at home and in far-ranging deployments, to assure that every member of the team is able to perform at peak efficiency in the event of crisis.

Chapter **VII**

The United States Naval Reserve

The Naval Reserve serves as a major portion of the U.S. Navy's overall readiness and operations capabilities. Tasked with providing trained units and individuals in the event of war or other national emergency, the Navy's Reserve component must keep its ranks filled with skilled men and women who are capable of serving with their Reserve unit upon mobilization or, if assigned to elements of the active force, performing effectively in units of the regular Navy. In the event of mobilization, about 20 percent of the Navy's personnel would be Reservists.

While the idea of a Naval Reserve had been discussed by government officials in the early 1800s and a number of state naval militias had been formed later in that century, it was not until 1915 that Congress authorized a Naval Reserve Force. A Naval Militia Act in 1914 had instructed states with naval militia in how to organize those units according to Navy Department plans; that helped to expedite formation of the Federal Naval Reserve when Congressional authorization was obtained.

More than 330,000 Naval Reservists served on active duty during World War I, including 12,000 women who served in Navy and Marine Corps office jobs. The Naval Reservists who served during that war performed with distinction and demonstrated the value of a well-trained Reserve force aboard ships and in aviation roles. When the United States entered World War II, most Naval Reservists had already been called to active duty. The number of personnel in the Reserve force had diminished substantially between World War I and World War II; however, by the end of the latter war most of the Navy's nearly three million men and women on active duty were Reservists.

Since World War II, Naval Reservists have continually trained and stood ready to respond to crisis. Many served on extended active duty or for shorter periods in Naval operations during the Korean and Vietnam Wars and in a number of other crises around the world, including several in the 1980s. The first naval officer to be awarded the nation's highest award for valor—the Medal of Honor—during the Vietnam War was a Naval Reserve chaplain who was killed in action while serving with a U.S. Marine infantry unit.

In the years since the end of the Vietnam War, the Naval Reserve has assumed an increased share of the overall responsibilities of the U.S. Navy, and the demand for talented men and women to serve as Reservists has grown accordingly.

Mobilization Requirements

Several categories of Naval Reservists are eligible for call should mobilization occur; most are in the ranks of drilling units of the Ready Reserve and are designated as members of the Selected Reserve. Substantial numbers of Naval Reservists are also serving on active duty at any given time, including several thousand who are assigned to the training and administration of the Reserve force or are serving with Naval Reserve ships and aircraft squadrons.

A young person entering the Naval Reserve with the intent of serving as an enlisted member of a drilling unit in or near his or her hometown becomes a member of the Selected Reserve, the core of the Navy's Reserve program. Members of the Selected Reserve are a source of immediate manpower in the event of mobilization. They normally perform one weekend of Reserve duty each month and two weeks of annual training duty each summer aboard a ship or naval base. Over the course of their service, they are paid for drills and annual training duty and any other active service they perform, and they earn the benefits, allowances, and points toward retirement afforded to all drilling Reservists. As members of the Selected Reserve they are subject to involuntary call to active duty in the event of mobilization.

They may also be called to involuntary active duty by the President for up to 90 days to support an operational requirement even though mobilization has not been put into effect and a national emergency has not been declared; such call-ups of Reserve forces are very rare.

Many members of the Naval Reserve are former members of the regular Navy who have chosen to retain their ties with the service while they pursue civilian careers. Many others, however, enlisted specifically for Reserve service and have served on active duty for training for periods of less than 180 days prior to reporting to their hometown unit for weekend drills and annual training duty.

The Navy's Sea and Air Mariner (SAM) program provides the Naval Reserve with recruits who have had no prior service; they usually begin service as junior enlisted personnel. Another Sea and Air Mariner program produces Reserve junior commissioned officers after a period of active duty training. A Reserve program called Reserve Allied Medical Personnel (RAMPS) offers free tuition at a two-year civilian college for persons entering Reserve service to be medical or dental technicians.

The Naval Reserve Officer Training Corps (NROTC) program offered at many colleges and universities provides a steady input of officers into Naval Reserve service. Participants are paid for undergoing service-related training during their college years, take part in summer cruises as part of the program, and are commissioned ensigns in the Naval Reserve or 2nd lieutenants in the Marine Corps Reserve upon graduation from college. Another source of Naval Reserve officers is the U.S. Merchant Marine Academy at Kings Point, New York. Graduates of that school usually enter commercial maritime service but also receive Naval Reserve commissions and may enter into active Navy or Coast Guard service. Navy recruiting offices and the NROTC offices at colleges and universities can provide information on the NROTC program; information on the Merchant Marine Academy may be obtained by writing to the U.S. Department of Transportation, Maritime Administration, Washington, DC 20590.

Generally, Reservists may qualify for the same specialties or technical fields available to members of the regular Navy. The ability to enter all fields, however, may be limited by the needs of the Navy at a given time. Navy recruiters can provide prospective Reservists with detailed information on available specialties and technical schools and programs. In some instances, students who qualify for Reserve service may be able to complete basic training during the summer between civilian school years. This may include training for seventeen-year-old high school students in the summer between their junior and senior years.

Element of the Total Force

In mobilization planning, the Navy relies on its Reserve force for a wide range of skilled personnel and substantial quantities of equipment. Even in peacetime the Naval Reserve maintains transport airlift squadrons, light attack helicopter squadrons, combat search and rescue aircraft, mobile inshore undersea warfare units, and carrier aircraft wings as part of the U.S. Navy's total force. The Reserve also provides a large segment of ocean minesweeping, cargo-handling, construction, special boat force, and military sealift personnel. In the event of war or other national emergency leading to a call-up, those units, personnel, and other Reserve-maintained assets are immediately available for service with the active force.

Should the Naval Reserve undergo such a call to active service, it can provide three types of combat-ready units: Commissioned units are those able to serve as a complete operational unit with the operating forces, having their own combat-ready equipment including ships; they may be aircraft squadrons, construction battalions, cargo-handling battalions, or other units. Reinforcing units are those that may be called on to augment active Navy units and operating staffs or united Marine Corps combat commands, they provide trained personnel to the units they augment. Sustaining units of the Naval Reserve would augment support activities with trained people who would help deal with the surge in buildup of forces at the time of mobilization and then help sustain support of deployed ships and units.

Some of the commissioned units of the Naval Reserve include ships such as destroyers, minesweepers, frigates, and amphibious ships; shore and support forces; squadrons of fixed-wing attack, fighter, patrol, and logistics support aircraft, and attack, antisubmarine warfare, and search and rescue helicopters. Reserve ships are manned by both active duty and Selected Reserve sailors and are based at more than a dozen home ports along the Pacific, Atlantic, and Gulf of Mexico

Naval Reserve personnel sometimes participate in amphibious operations in which Marine Reservists are transported to coastal areas and moved ashore by sea or air.

coasts. Naval Air Reserve squadrons are based at about twenty locations around the country, with most at air stations, bases, or air facilities in or near coastal regions. Some air stations operated by the Reserve would become fleet operational bases upon mobilization.

The Naval Reserve operates about 250 training sites nationwide. Most are Reserve centers and facilities used to train the reinforcing and sustaining units of the Naval Surface Reserve Force. Many of the centers are equipped with shipboard simulators that permit Reservists to train under many of the conditions they would face aboard ship, far at sea. Because of the availability and use of simulators, sailors reporting for active duty following mobilization will be better prepared to solve problems relating to communications, damage control, power generation, and other routine or emergency operating procedures. Additionally, Naval Reservists are often transported to locations other than their local training site for specialized training to improve the force's overall combat readiness.

Drills and Other Service

To illustrate the diversity of Naval Reserve service, the following is a composite of actual training and operational activities carried out by Naval Reservists at various times in recent years. The examples are described in the present tense for illustration only:

- During one twelve-month period, Naval Reserve squadrons fly more than 640 hours of surveillance flights in support of a drug interdiction program directed by the Vice President of the United States. During that same year, Naval Reserve construction forces contribute 21,000 man-days of mutual support to active duty Navy and Marine Corps commands.
- When the space shuttle *Challenger* is lost in an explosion immediately after liftoff, Naval Reservists volunteer for duty aboard search vessels. A Reservist locates the crew compartment.

- A Reserve carrier air wing embarked aboard a regular force carrier conducts day and night training operations for extended periods against shore targets more than 1,000 miles away. Meanwhile, Naval Reservists volunteer for duty aboard the battleship USS Iowa when it is supporting U.S. forces operating in Lebanon.

- During a time of increased international tension in Central America, Naval Reserve ships operate in nearby waters as a part of an operation to illustrate U.S. concern for events in the region. With nearly 22,000 hours of flight time, Reserve aviators perform all of the fleet logistics support within the continental U.S. during an entire year; at the same time, surface force Reservists provide more than 100,000 man-days of support to fleet exercises. Also within a 12-month period, 44 weeks of fleet support are provided by Reserve squadrons from around the country in support of U.S. bases in the Azores and Japan.

- When U.S. and allied interests are threatened during the war between Iraq and Iran, Naval Reserve ships are among those sent to the Persian Gulf for extensive patrols. Tasked to reach the gulf quickly, two guided missile frigates and five minesweepers of the Naval Reserve Force move to their assigned positions without being delayed for upgrading of equipment or additional crew training. Reservists belonging to special boat units also volunteer for surveillance duty in the mined channels of the Persian Gulf. At about the same time, large numbers of Naval Reservists are participating in fleet exercises in Scotland, England, and Norway and providing shore and air logistics support for NATO forces in the Norwegian Sea.

- During floods along the coast of the Gulf of Mexico, Naval Reservists assist civil authorities in rescue and disaster relief operations. In a different type of lifesaving operation, Naval Reserve aircraft equipped to detect the movement of ships and aircraft are used on drug interdiction flights in support of other federal agencies, and several Naval Reserve ships participate in operations designed to curb the flow of illegal drugs into the U.S.

- On the West Coast, a Reserve carrier air wing conducts annual training duty aboard a nuclear-powered aircraft carrier. Reserve pilots refine their skills in takeoffs and landings from a floating base; other Naval Reservists qualify to perform as members of flight deck crews.
- Naval Reservists from forward freight terminal support units participate in the movement of a 1,000-bed rapidly deployable field hospital from a ship anchored off Yokosuka, Japan, to a U.S. Army facility near the city. The 150 participating Reservists are expected to complete the job in eight days; they get it done in six. Before leaving Japan the sailors visit Japanese cities and historic sites. Several hundred miles to the south, dozens of Naval Reserve doctors, dentists, nurses, and hospital corpsmen serve aboard a hospital ship during its five-month deployment to the Philippines.
- Reservists at a number of Naval Reserve training sites nationwide begin receiving special instruction in the use of new high technology–based administration equipment, including the latest in personal computers. In addition to using their new skills in their own duty assignments, they will help train other members of their unit on the new systems during weekend drills and on annual training duty.
- In a similar situation—but this time with sophisticated operational equipment—Naval Reservists work with members of the active force and technical representatives from an aircraft manufacturing company in developing maintenance procedures for a new type of helicopter scheduled to enter service. Upon completion of training, the Reservists will be capable of supporting a squadron of the new aircraft in search and rescue missions and special operations.

Part-time Service in a Full-time Force

Service in the Naval Reserve is not always just a matter of reporting for drill two days a month and serving on active duty for two weeks each summer. All of the foregoing Reserve activities and support operations were carried out during drill weekends, annual training duty, or when individual Reservists or units volunteered for service in response to special situations.

The U.S. Navy has established a reputation for operating some of the best technical schools in the world. Graduates of its electronics, communications, avionics, and other technological courses have not only helped sustain the operational capabilities of the Navy's surface and air forces but have also moved into key positions in private industry. Many specialties, of course, do not require extensive technological skills. In evaluating prospective Naval Reservists, recruiting personnel look at test scores, educational background, and other factors that comprise an individual's potential. Assignment to specialty schools is based on that evaluation, the specialties of interest to the applicant, and the needs of the service.

Once assigned to a nearby Naval Reserve unit, a Reservist may find that his or her naval specialty can lead to some faraway locations—even on drill weekends—when special skills are needed for a short time. As the examples cited earlier demonstrate, a Reservist may also be offered the opportunity to volunteer for active duty for an extended period to assist in an emergency situation close to home or halfway around the world.

In taking on more and more operational commitments over the past few years, the Naval Reserve has become an increasingly vital link in the overall network that comprises the Navy's total force. Reservists contribute directly or indirectly to every aspect of naval operations. Counterterrorism briefings, intelligence-gathering and investigative support, substantial blocks of medical support, assistance in fleet exercises, flight instruction for student naval aviators, reconnaissance missions by Reserve squadrons—all are carried out by Naval Reservists not only on drill weekends and annual training duty but throughout the year.

The Naval Reserve has been assigned to provide 100 percent of the total Navy capability in several functional areas. During one recent year Reservists were responsible for all of the

Navy's fleet logistics aircraft, light attack helicopters, combat search and rescue aircraft, and mobile inshore undersea warfare units.

Because of their demonstrated ability and willingness to respond to so many unusual situations, one Chief of Naval Reserve described Naval Reservists as an essential element of the Navy and national defense who can appropriately be called "part-time regulars." In the event of mobilization, more than 2,500 reinforcing and sustaining units of the Naval Reserve would provide the Total Force with skilled personnel in a large number of specialties. Young men and women entering the Naval Reserve can expect to be trained on some of the best equipment in the world—and then to put their training to use at locations not only at home but worldwide over the course of their service.

Chapter VIII

The United States Marine Corps Reserve

The effectiveness of any country's Reserve forces depends on their ability to mobilize and undertake specific responsibilities that usually have been determined well in advance of mobilization. Like the other U.S. Reserve forces, the Marine Corps Reserve was designed and developed to carry out a smooth and rapid transition to active duty in times of national crisis.

The U.S. Marine Corps was created in 1775 and in the course of its more than 200 years has earned a reputation for often being the first service called upon when an immediate response is needed to counter threats to the United States, its citizens, or its national interests.

In the late 1800s, when some coastal states established naval militias, Marine detachments were formed in conjunction with some of them. Those Marine detachments were, in effect, Reserve units and are now considered forerunners of the Marine Corps Reserve, which was formally established by an act of Congress in 1916. Shortly after its establishment, the Marine Corps Reserve was providing men for combat service in World War I. By the end of that war in 1918, nearly 7,000 Marine Reservists were on active duty and many had served in ground or aerial combat in France. In World War II Marine Reservists again contributed significantly. Of the nearly 500,000 Marines who served in battle during the course of that war, more than two thirds were Reservists. Marine Reservists were also among the first troops to be deployed from the United States to the combat zone during the Korean conflict in the early 1950s, and several thousand served in Vietnam.

Full-time Partners in Readiness

The Marine Corps Reserve is a full partner, with its active force counterpart, in what the Marines often call themselves— the nation's Force-in-Readiness. More than 43,000 Marine Reservists serve in either the 4th Marine Division or the 4th Marine Aircraft Wing, the two major Reserve force combat elements. The 4th Division Wing-Team trains continuously to maintain a high state of combat readiness and to assure that mobilization can occur quickly. Upon mobilization, the Marine Corps Reserve would comprise 25 percent of the Corps' total fighting power and nearly a third of its total personnel.

Reservists who train during drill weekends at more than 180 Reserve training centers around the nation and at major military installations during annual training duty are members of the Selected Marine Corps Reserve. Another category of Marine Reservists, the Individual Ready Reserve, is composed of 44,000 Marines who have completed periods of active duty and are trained in military specialties but do not attend weekend or summer training periods. They are, however, on call in the event of national emergency and can be recalled to active duty until such time as they have fulfilled their obligated active and Reserve service. (In 1991, as a result of federal legislation, individual military service obligation will become eight years.)

Individual Mobilization Augmentees make up a third category of Marine Reservists; they are drilling Reservists who train with active duty counterparts in preassigned positions that they would fill in the event of mobilization. These individual Reservists are usually assigned to positions at Marine Corps bases and air station, staff headquarters, and mobilization stations. The IMAs fill important positions, and Corps leaders point with pride to the fact that some of them served in the Marine Corps Command Center when U.S. troops landed on

Grenada in the early 1980s to remove Cuban forces and return control of the island nation to its people.

Members of the Selected Marine Corps Reserve use their drill weekends and annual training duty for individual and unit training. Field exercises with other Reserve units and active forces help assure that both personnel and equipment are always ready for mobilization. The Marine Corps places special emphasis on Marine Air-Ground Task Force training in which ground and air units train as teams. These task forces often operate with the Navy to conduct amphibious warfare training in which Marines and their weapons and equipment put to sea and then participate in simulated assaults on objectives ashore.

Exercises are also used to train Marine Reserve ground units in the employment of artillery, naval gunfire, and air support. To assure that combat units are able to perform under a wide range of conditions and situations, training may focus on mountain warfare, jungle operations, cold-weather operations, and situations relating to battle conditions involving nuclear, biological, and chemical weapons. In addition to training at local sites during drill weekends and at major military installations in the U.S. during annual training duty, many Marine Reservists train at overseas locations each year.

Marine Reservists are generally equipped with the same weapons and equipment employed by the regular forces; however, in some instances—particularly in aviation—the Reserves may continue to use items that have been phased out or are being phased out by the regular component. The Reserves are, however, equipped in such a way that will permit their total integration into active force units without being hampered by differences in ammunition, spare parts, or special maintenance requirements.

Marine Reserve Service

Persons may enter the Marine Corps Reserve directly through enlistment or officer commissioning programs, or they may enter after completing active service contracts as members of the regular Marine Corps.

The initial period of active duty for someone who enlists specifically as a Marine Reservist generally is six months. That includes twelve weeks of recruit training (which Marines refer to as boot camp), followed by specialty training at a formal school or on-the-job training with an active force unit. Recruit training for male Marines takes place at either Parris Island, South Carolina, or San Diego, California. Recruit training for women Marines is conducted only at Parris Island.

Boot camp for Marines is designed to produce a basic "warrior." That is to say, everyone earning the title "U.S. Marine" is expected not only to be able to perform specific tasks relating to a military specialty but also to be proficient in other purely military skills. All male Marines must possess the skills needed to participate effectively in offensive and defensive combat operations; women Marines, although not trained for combat, are required to master certain security-related tasks in addition to skills associated with their military occupational specialty.

Persons may earn Reserve commissions in the Marines through Naval Reserve Officer Training Corps programs at colleges and universities; by entering commissioning programs upon graduation from college; and through programs available to active and Reserve enlisted Marines. Almost all Marine officers except those commissioned following graduation from the service academies attend an officer candidate school before assignment to The Basic School, the Corps' leadership training center for newly commissioned officers at Quantico, Virginia. Commissioning as a Reserve officer is usually followed by an extended period of active service. Following active service, many Reserve officers choose to maintain their ties with the Marine Corps by serving with Reserve units near their home. Some end their Reserve career when their civilian career or other situations will not permit continued service; others are able to continue their Reserve career until meeting or exceeding the minimum service needed to qualify for retirement benefits.

Unit Training

Once an enlisted Reserve Marine has completed recruit training and the initial active duty phase of his or her service obligation, the remainder of obligated service is usually carried out with a Marine Reserve unit in or near the city in which the Reservist lives. Most monthly drill periods are conducted at or near the Reserve training center; mandatory annual training duty is generally carried out at major military bases in the U.S. Annual training duty, however, may include participation in training exercises at overseas locations. In one recent year, 22,000 Marine Reservists were transported to foreign locations to participate in major exercises with active force Marines and allied military units.

Once a Marine Reservist returns home upon completion of initial training, exactly what does he or she do relative to the military obligation? The Marine Corps offers four Reserve enlistment programs, each of which offers a different number of years spent in a full drill status; during the full drill period, Reservists perform one drill weekend each month and attend annual training duty for two weeks each year. After completing full drill service, the Reservist moves into the Individual Ready Reserve and is liable to call-up in an emergency but attends no drills or annual training duty.

Weekend drill periods and annual training duty are as varied as are the occupational specialties and types of units throughout the Marine Corps Reserve. Following are examples of activities that have actually taken place at Marine Reserve training centers and at major bases during annual training duty in the recent past. Activities are described in the present tense for illustration only:

- Weapons Company, 1st Battalion, 24th Marine Regiment operates from a Reserve training center in Toledo, Ohio; the infantry unit spends the majority of its drill periods in areas remote from its training center. The Toledo Marines have been involved in field training for as many as nine of

Every Marine—regular or Reservist—undergoes basic warrior training before being assigned a specialty.

their twelve drill weekends in one year. Some of the field weekends take them on three-hour rides to Fort Custer, Michigan, for cold-weather training. Winter visits to Fort Custer often involve setting up tents and operating from base camps in subzero weather. Specially equipped for cold-weather operations, the Toledo Reservists learn to operate using snowshoes and arctic boots while carrying fully loaded packs, individual weapons, and crew-served weapons such as mortars and machine guns over several miles of snow-covered trails and forest trails.

- Meanwhile, a few hundred miles away, Marine Reservists from an aviation unit undergo cold-weather training at Fort McCoy, Wisconsin. They endure under even colder weather conditions than those faced by the Toledo unit but, instead of having to march over miles of snow, their assignment is to learn how to overcome problems that arise in maintaining and operating light helicopters in extreme cold. Their training is in preparation for participation in major international military exercises in Norway.

- The annual training duty of Marine Reservists is usually carried out with their unit during the summer—but not always. A Marine Fighter Attack Squadron from Washington, D.C., completes its annual training duty during the winter—but not in the frigid northern U.S. or Scandinavia. The squadron, with more than 300 of its Reservists and nearly 100 active duty Marines who support the unit, deploy to the Naval Air Station at Miramar, California, and the Marine Corps Air Station at El Toro, California. Pilots and radar intercept officers of the squadron practice aerial tactics—averaging seventeen missions per day—at southern California bases and ranges while maintenance, supply, and administrative personnel support them from ground installations.

- The examples so far have covered instances of annual training duty during winter months; however, it is more common for Marine Reserve units to carry out that duty during the summer.

In the not-too-distant past a Marine Reservist could very well count on spending his or her annual training duty at Camp Pendleton, California, Camp Lejeune, North Carolina, or one of the Marine Corps' air stations in the U.S. With the increasing importance of the Reserve components of all of the Armed Forces, however, training at home locations and annual training duty have become more intense and more varied. A Marine Reserve light antiaircraft missile battalion from Glenview, Illinois, for example, may participate in two weeks of firing exercises over U.S. Army ranges at Dugway Proving Grounds near Salt Lake City, Utah. Instead of simulating the firing of Hawk missiles as they had frequently been required to do in the past, they are able to fire their air defense missiles at drones (unmanned, remotely controlled aircraft) far down-range.

For Marine Reservists in Hawk missile battalions and other units that train to employ sophisticated weapons, the firing of live missiles and other ordnance is very important in developing skills, assuring proficiency, and building unit and individual self-confidence. Just as important is realistic training and proficiency evaluation for Marine Reservists in all other specialties. Without practicing both the fundamentals and the more complex aspects of their specialties, individuals and units would have to undergo additional training before becoming effective in the event of mobilization.

Often, the general public visualizes Marines only in terms of infantry troops storming ashore in landing craft to seize enemy positions while supported by Marine pilots flying attack and fighter aircraft. Indeed, amphibious warfare and the seizure of terrain from enemy hands are part of the Corps' overall mission. But to get infantry Marines and Marine pilots to their objective area, to assure that they can communicate with each other and with supporting aircraft and ships, and to be certain that they have enough ammunition and equipment to accomplish their mission, thousands of other Marines must serve in supporting roles. For that reason, many Reserve units are established to provide support in the event of combat operations; and even within combat units a certain number of personnel are always assigned to support roles such as administration and supply. Therefore, a person interested in the Marine Corps Reserve but not interested in serving in combat arms specialties may find other positions available in a combat arms unit; or the nearest Marine Reserve unit may be a support unit that offers many positions in technical fields.

The potential Marine Reservist must keep two things in mind, however. First, every male Marine is considered a rifleman and may be called upon to perform as such if the needs of national defense dictate. A certain portion of training for active force and Reserve Marines is set aside each year to assure that all male Marines will be able to function effectively as infan-

Marine Corps and Naval Reservists may be trained in many specialties, including flight deck operations and aircraft maintenance.

trymen in combat situations. Second, each Marine serving in other than a combat arms role is serving for one basic purpose: to help assure that every Marine entering combat is able to carry out his mission successfully.

In all, Marine Corps Reservists serve in more than 300 specialties grouped within the following occupational fields:

Air Control Air Support/Anti-Air Warfare
Air Traffic Control and Enlisted Flight Crews
Aircraft Maintenance
Airfield Services
Ammunition and Explosive Ordnance Disposal
Auditing, Finance, Accounting
Aviation Ordnance
Avionics
Data/Communications Maintenance
Data Systems
Drafting, Surveying, and Mapping
Electronics Maintenance
Engineer, Construction, Equipment, and Shore Party
Field Artillery
Food Service
Infantry
Intelligence
Legal Services
Logistics
Marine Corps Exchange
Military Police and Corrections
Motor Transport
Nuclear, Biological, and Chemical
Operational Communications
Ordnance
Personnel and Administration
Printing and Reproduction
Public Affairs
Signal Intelligence/Ground Electronic Warfare
Supply Administration and Operations

Tank and Amphibian Tractor
Training and Audiovisual Support
Transportation
Utilities
Weather Service

The foregoing occupational fields indicate the broad range of specialties in which Marine Reservists perform, both at home training facilities and when operating with the active force. Many of the fields are self-explanatory in their titles, but others do not fully describe the types of specialties within their scope. Public affairs, for example, encompasses journalism, photo-journalism, electronic (radio and television) newsgathering, and public relations. Intelligence includes photo interpretation, terrain analysis, counterintelligence, interrogation techniques, and other activities that help Marines identify, locate, and engage enemy forces. Data/communications maintenance involves making sure that radios, Teletypes, and other types of electronic equipment are operable and in a continued state of readiness when not in use. Logistics means outfitting Marines with weapons, ammunition, water, food, and other essential supplies; moving all those items when they need to be moved; and assuring that medical supplies and care are available when and where they are needed.

The foregoing are just some examples of fields—and specialties within fields—that must be filled by qualified Marine Reservists on a sustained basis. To reach the levels of training needed to operate effectively, Reservists may attend service schools during initial active duty and at certain periods over the course of their service. The skills gained from such schools and on-the-job application of what they have learned in weekend drills and annual training duty are combined to produce effective units capable of performing as teams.

As one senior Marine officer has stated, the degree of success in integrating Reserve units and individual Reservists into the active force in the event of mobilization will ultimately be determined on the battlefield. For that reason, the Marine

Corps continually seeks the most highly qualified young men and women it can find to fill the ranks of the Marine Corps Reserve.

Chapter IX

The United States Coast Guard Reserve

The Coast Guard Reserve was established in 1941 and reached a wartime active duty strength of more than 140,000 during World War II; another 45,000 Coast Guard Temporary Reservists performed port security work during that war. It was not until almost five years after World War II ended that organized drilling units of paid Coast Guard Reservists began to be formed.

Today the Coast Guard Reserve mission is to provide trained units and individuals to serve on active duty in the event of war or national emergency and to help fill the needs of the regular Coast Guard when more units or individuals are required than are available in the active force. Reservists represent nearly a quarter of the total manpower of the Coast Guard.

Unlike the other Armed Forces, the Coast Guard is not a part of the Department of Defense during peacetime. It is an agency of the U.S. Department of Transportation. In wartime and other periods designated by the President the Coast Guard serves in the Department of the Navy.

Among the Coast Guard's peacetime responsibilities are security of America's ports and waterways, maritime law enforcement, maritime search and rescue, commercial vessel safety, and polar and domestic icebreaking. Most of those duties would be continued in the event of war, but port security operations would be expanded. Additionally, the Coast Guard would take on other assignments designated by the U.S. Navy, many relating to protection of the coastal regions that are defined within Maritime Defense Zones. Defense of those zones would be undertaken by regulars and Reserves of the Coast Guard and Navy.

Because of the special relationship between the Coast Guard and the Navy, Coast Guard personnel—regular and Reserve—must continually be prepared to make a rapid and smooth transition into the Department of the Navy in the event of war.

Training

Members of the Coast Guard's Selected Reserve are trained in specific skills that would be needed by the active force in the event of mobilization. Training in those skills is conducted during a Reservist's recruit training, during specialty training at formal schools or on the job immediately following recruit training, and throughout the Reservist's career in weekend drills and on annual training duty. Most Coast Guard Reservists carry out weekend and annual training duty with active force Coast Guard units that are fulfilling peacetime missions. In this, Coast Guard Reservists differ from their counterparts in the other Armed Forces, where the majority of Reservists usually participate in weekend drills and annual training duty with only their organized Reserve unit.

About two thirds of all Coast Guard Reserve training is carried out in support of active Coast Guard programs and operations. Thus, Reservists are directly involved in port security inspections, safety and environmental inspections and operations, and observation of the transfer and handling of hazardous material and petroleum by commercial and naval vessels. Reservists also spend weekend drills at Coast Guard search and rescue stations, where they stand watch, man communications systems, and participate in actual search and rescue operations. Some Reservists also work with elements of the active force aboard Coast Guard cutters and other vessels.

Members of the Coast Guard Reserve often augment their parent service in operations during and following natural disasters. Reservists may be called on to stand watch or participate in rescues during hurricanes, floods, or other times when life and property are threatened. They are also often called upon to respond to maritime disasters such as fires, oil spills, and collisions of vessels in ports, harbors, and coastal regions.

Training for Coast Guard Reservists is designed to prepare them for maritime defense, security, and safety operations. In addition to evaluation in the course of routine training weekends, skill levels are also monitored while Reservists are participating in major exercises with the Coast Guard and the other Armed Forces. Reservists are offered the same specialties available to members of the active force as well as two additional ones—data processing and port security.

Missions

Reservists must be prepared to mobilize and move into positions with the active Coast Guard as expeditiously as possible in the event of war or other national emergency. The missions of the active Coast Guard are therefore the same missions for which its Reserve personnel must prepare through training.

The Coast Guard's role in defense is important both in peacetime and in war. The service participates regularly in programs with the other Armed Forces, in U.S. fleet exercises, and in other training maneuvers involving American and allied forces. The Coast Guard has played key roles as an arm of the Navy in every major conflict involving U.S. forces, including World War II, Korea, and Vietnam. During such crises, the Coast Guard has participated with distinction in search and rescue, port safety and security, amphibious operations, and many other tasks.

As important as the Coast Guard's defense mission is, the service is probably more familiar to the general public for its efforts in boating safety and in search and rescue operations. Boating has become a favorite form of recreation, and with the pleasure has come a need for search and rescue services to deal with disasters at sea and on the nation's waterways. Since the early 1970s the Coast Guard has conducted a national boating safety program, which includes research on boating equipment and establishment and monitoring of safety standards both on the water and in production of equipment.

The service has helped create some of the best boating education programs available and has worked extensively with state and other federal agencies to enhance public safety on the water. Many present and past members of the Coast Guard and Coast Guard Reserve gained initial exposure to their service through instruction received from a Coast Guard–related activity at the local level. That activity—the Coast Guard Auxiliary—has become an important contributor to the Guard's overall boating safety program. It is a civilian volunteer organization of several thousand men and women dedicated to providing educational and boating safety services to recreational boaters.

When proper safety procedures have not been applied by boaters and operators of commercial vessels, disaster can occur, and at such times one of the Coast Guard's most visible missions is carried out. In responding to nearly 100,000 calls for assistance in water-related incidents each year, the Coast Guard saves thousands of lives and assists many thousands of other people in distress at sea or on lakes and rivers. In one recent year more than $400,000 worth of property was saved as a result of Coast Guard rescue missions. The service is on watch continually and prepared day or night to launch rescue and assistance teams by boat, helicopter, and fixed-wing aircraft.

Part of the search and rescue mission is conducted from more than twenty-five Coast Guard air stations. The service also participates in an international search and rescue program, the Automated Mutual-assistance Vessel Rescue Program, which works with volunteer merchant vessels in providing aid to vessels at sea. Another aspect of search and rescue operations is the Coast Guard's participation in the International Ice Patrol, a service initiated following the sinking of the *Titanic*. The Coast Guard works with the services of other countries in patrolling 45,000 square miles of sea, sometimes tracking more than 1,000 icebergs during a single year.

One of the Coast Guard's oldest missions is providing and maintaining aids to navigation. Among the navigational aids, serviced and maintained by a fleet of Coast Guard ships, are hundreds of lighthouses and several thousand minor navigation lights that help the crews of boats and ships determine their position and steer clear of dangerous areas. These navigation lights are positioned along well-traveled waterways, on or near prominent terrain features along coastlines, on or near shipping hazards, and at the entrances to major bodies of water. In all, the Coast Guard maintains nearly 50,000 aids to navigation, including thousands of buoys. Two types of electronic aids to navigation operated by the service are LORAN-C and OMEGA. These systems transmit signals that are received by boats and ships and used by crews to determine their position.

Another Coast Guard mission is to serve as a regulatory agency for America's merchant fleet. It monitors all aspects of merchant shipping operations from approval of the design and construction of vessels, to their operation and, ultimately, their disposal when they are no longer serviceable. Operators of merchant vessels must be licensed by the Coast Guard and are subject to penalties when they fail to operate within prescribed guidelines. The service inspects ships for safety, serviceability, presence of required lifesaving and safety equipment, and proper storage and movement of cargo. In the event of serious shipping accidents, the Coast Guard is responsible for conducting investigations to determine the causes.

A mission with which Coast Guard Reservists have become increasingly familiar in recent years has been environmental protection. Reservists participating in drill weekends with members of the regular force sometimes deal with oil spills and other contaminants in waterways. The Coast Guard has been responsible for developing environmental protection regulations—and enforcing them—for nearly 100 years. At major oil spills such as the one in Alaska's Prince William Sound in 1989, and in other incidents involving the accidental discharge of hazardous materials, the Coast Guard works with government agencies, the oil and shipping industries, and other parties affected by the incidents to reduce damage and clean waterways to the extent possible. The Coast Guard maintains strike teams made up of pollution control, diving, marine salvage, and other specialists who are prepared to be flown to major spill sites on very short notice.

Port safety is another major task carried out by the Coast Guard. It protects shipping and port facilities from accidents as well as sabotage and other subversive activities. This mission is conducted from the service's Marine Safety and Captain-of-the-Port offices. Ships are inspected for conformity with safety regulations and to determine that cargo is stored safely. In the case of hazardous cargo, handling procedures are monitored and supervised.

Of growing importance to the country is the Coast Guard's maritime law enforcement operations. For many years those missions related primarily to general maritime law enforcement and marine safety. Today, however, the Coast Guard is on the leading edge of the war against drug smuggling, and that duty occupies a large percentage of day-to-day operations. This includes inspection of commercial vessels and pleasure craft for cargoes of illegal drugs, the tracking of ships and aircraft to prevent the movement of illegal drugs, and the apprehension of drug smugglers.

Within all of the foregoing Coast Guard missions are dozens of requirements that require special skills. Members of the Coast Guard Reserve are often called upon during drill periods and annual training duty to apply their skills alongside members of the active force to accomplish those missions.

Reserve Service Programs

Among programs offered by the Coast Guard is the Reserve Summer Jobs Program, in which high school, college, or vocational school students conduct their initial active duty training over two summers. For young people at least seventeen and enrolled in high school, it permits completion of Coast Guard recruit training the summer before their senior year. Whether the student is in high school, college, or trade school, regular studies are not interrupted, and weekend drills during the final academic year are for only one day each month with the local Reserve unit. In addition to being paid during recruit training, the participant is also paid for the weekend drills and receives other normal benefits of Reserve service such as low cost life insurance.

Upon mobilization, a Coast Guard Reservist could be assigned to any of a number of duties, including positioning and maintenance of navigational aids.

The second summer of participation in the program provides the individual with specialty training and possibly a formal service school. Following that training, the Reservist returns home to pursue his or her civilian career and continue participation in monthly drills and annual training duty with the Coast Guard Reserve for the remainder of a specific period of obligated service. One advantage of participation in this program is the additional income, which may help pay the costs of higher education or be used for other personal interests. Participants in the program also qualify for tuition assistance and other programs available to Reservists.

Another special training program available in the Coast Guard Reserve is the Petty Officer Selectee Program, in which participants undergo thirty weeks of recruit and advanced training, with schooling guaranteed. Also available to persons who have graduated from school and gained civilian work experience in skills needed by the Coast Guard is the Direct Petty Officer Program, under which an individual can enter the Reserve force at a rank higher than recruit level. Among other special Reserve programs are one for persons with prior military service and another in which a person may qualify for a direct commission.

Skills and Jobs

Persons entering the Coast Guard Reserve often are assigned to formal schools during their initial active duty training to prepare them for the job they will perform in their specialty upon returning to their home unit. Once back at the home unit, drills are generally as varied as are the types of missions performed by the active Coast Guard. Drills are usually performed on weekends.

Where a Coast Guard Reservist lives plays an important part in the type of assignment he or she may expect. Those living at or near major ports can expect to be frequently involved in port security, monitoring of cargo operations, and environmental protection. In areas where illegal drug operations are taking place, a Reservist may become involved in helping to interdict the flow of drugs. Where commercial fishing operations are an important part of regional commerce, Reservists may work with their active duty counterparts in protecting against poaching by foreign vessels.

Since the Coast Guard is deeply involved in search and rescue operations on a routine basis, a Reservist may spend weekend drills at a search and rescue station, working with recreational boaters, and maintaining navigational aids. When civil disasters such as floods, hurricanes, and maritime fires occur, Coast Guard Reservists may also become involved in the response by assisting in the security of property and businesses and in lifesaving operations. At the Kennedy Space Center in Florida, Coast Guard Reservists frequently man small boats that patrol an area of more than 140 square miles around the launch site to monitor the thousands of private craft that fill the waterways on launch days. The Reservists are involved in security of the site as well as providing search and rescue services.

Another type of duty in which a Coast Guard Reservist may become involved during drill periods is firefighting in or near waterways. Reservists have been instrumental in stopping the spread of fires in and around major oil storage areas and in controlling spills caused by such fires adjacent to waterways.

While the Coast Guard is the smallest of the nation's armed forces, its responsibilities are significant. And because of the small size of the active force, the Coast Guard Reserve plays a key role in the overall operations and mobilization readiness of the parent service. Frequently drill periods are not taken up only by training sessions but involve participation in important operations relating to national maritime safety and security.

In addition to work with water craft, Reservists who live near Coast Guard aviation facilities may become involved in operations relating to use of the service's fixed-wing aircraft and helicopters. Coast Guard aviation units monitor waterways and coastal zones to help preserve life and property and to guard against illegal activities.

Coast Guard Reservists earn the same pay and benefits as members of the other Reserve components. Their unique service, however, sets them apart and provides frequent opportunities to contribute to the well-being of the community. Whether involved in lifesaving, pollution control, port security, or any number of other routine assignments or called upon to assist the active force in emergency situations, members of the Coast Guard Reserve represent an important part of the national defense. They remain continually ready to respond not only in the event of national mobilization but also in many of the recurring crises faced by a maritime nation.

Part 3

RESERVE SERVICE AND
RESERVE CAREERS

Chapter X

Balancing Service, Career, and Family Life

The mission of United States Reserve forces, an individual's commitment to serve in those forces, and the operational requirements of each of the Reserve components are all elements that must be considered by individual Reservists from the day they enter service until the day their enlistment expires or they retire from a Reserve career. A Reservist must be prepared to balance military service, civilian employment, and family life—including educational commitments.

In the end, all those elements should be mutually supportive. They must be if the Reservist is to be an effective part of U.S. Reserve forces that are efficient, capable of rapid mobilization, and combat ready upon mobilization

Planning for Mobilization

One of the realities of Reserve service is that the members train continually for something they hope won't happen—mobilization. To fully understand the importance of balancing all aspects of one's civilian life and military obligations during Reserve service requires a clear understanding of just what mobilization is.

Mobilization may be in response to hostile action or anticipated hostile action by another country or countries against the United States and/or its allies; or it may be for some other reason, including a domestic emergency, that requires an increase in the number of persons on active duty in the armed forces. It is the process whereby a country expands its active armed forces very quickly. Among the most important aspects of mobilization is the calling of eligible Reservists to active duty. It may also involve increasing the tempo of recruiting volunteers for active service and instituting an induction process under which persons with no prior service may be voluntarily or involuntarily drafted into the armed forces.

In addition to increasing the number of military personnel on active duty, other national resources are prepared for possible use in the emergency, and a number of steps are taken by the government to increase domestic security. If mobilization is carried out in response to a domestic emergency, Reservists may be called on to protect life, property, and U.S. government institutions and activities.

Reserve units and individual Reservists who are mobilized are said to be called up. Unit members may be notified by telephone that they are being called to active service, with official notification following in the form of written orders received by mail or at the local Reserve training center. In past instances of mobilization it has not been uncommon for Reservists to first become aware of the call-up from news reports.

When Reservists or Reserve units are mobilized, the duration of active service varies with the situation. The government may specify a period of time; however, the actual time of service may be longer or shorter depending on the situation and on the part of federal law under which the mobilization was carried out.

Within the Department of Defense, the Joint Chiefs of Staff have established four levels of mobilization: selective, partial, full, and total mobilization.

Selective mobilization includes expansion of the armed forces as a result of action by Congress and/or the President to mobilize Reserve component units, individual Ready Reservists, and the resources needed for their support. Selective mobilization is undertaken in domestic emergencies.

Partial mobilization is the expansion of the active forces as a result of action by Congress to reach a level just short of full mobilization. It may also be action by the President to mobilize up to one million persons including entire Ready Reserve Component units and individual Reservists, and provision of resources needed to meet the requirements of a war or other emergency involving an external threat to national security.

Full mobilization is expansion of the active forces as a result of action taken by Congress and the President to mobilize all Reserve units in the existing force structure, all individual Reservists, and retired military personnel and assembling the resources needed to support them in a war or other national emergency involving an external threat. The existing approved force structure may include units that are not fully manned or equipped during peacetime but are to be filled in the event of mobilization.

Total mobilization is the expansion of active forces by Congress and the President to organize and/or establish additional units or increase personnel levels beyond the existing force structure and provide resources needed for their support in war or other emergency involving an external threat to national security.

The President may also, without Congressional action, take steps to augment the active force for any operational mission and order to involuntary active duty for not more than 90 days any Reserve unit and any Reservist not assigned to a unit organized to serve as part of the Selected Reserve. No more than 100,000 Reservists may serve on active duty under such a Presidential call-up at any one time.

As indicated in the foregoing definitions of mobilization and Presidential call-up, not all Reserve units and Reservists are necessarily called up in the event of mobilization. The number of individuals and units called are based on the national interests as determined by the President and Congress, who act on recommendations of the Secretary of Defense and the Joint Chiefs of Staff.

Types of mobilization and length of active service by Reservists upon mobilization vary according to very detailed specifications that are established under federal law.

Mobilization and Family

For an individual Reservist called to active duty as a result of mobilization, the time between call-up and reporting to an active force unit will vary depending on the nature of the emergency. In some circumstances, a Reservist may be able to spend several days taking care of personal affairs; however, the usual seriousness of situations leading to mobilization make that unlikely.

Once Reservists report to the unit in response to call-up for mobilization, there may be a period of time in which evenings may be spent at home as the unit prepares for departure to a major military installation or other location. But the very nature of mobilization dictates that Reservists not count on anything but short periods of time prior to departure.

That means that families must always be prepared to deal with the sudden absence of the Reservist for short or long periods of time. The leaders and administrative staffs of Reserve units help Reservists prepare for such situations and provide planning guidance that can greatly reduce the burden placed on families who must be left behind.

For planning purposes, the period immediately after call-up may be expected to be spent preparing equipment for movement and taking certain administrative actions required in mobilization. This is not always possible, however. In past mobilizations Reservists called to active duty were on the front lines and engaged in action against hostile forces before some active force units arrived in the combat zone. Unit commanders encourage Reservists to be prepared to depart on very short notice.

Preparation of family members to cope with the absence of a Reservist upon mobilization must begin early in the Reservist's military career. This is done by periodically reminding the family of the procedures that will occur in the event of call-up, being sure that personal affairs are in order at all times, and conducting a continuing education program relating to Reserve training and service.

Mobilization and Employer

Not only do members of the Reserve have a responsibility to prepare their families for the possibility of a sudden and prolonged absence, but they should also prepare their employers. The civilian employment of a Reservist who is mobilized is protected by federal law; however, to make things easier for everyone concerned the Reservist should discuss mobilization and all its implications with his or her employer. Most employers will support their employees called away in the event of mobilization. But sudden or prolonged absence—even for a national emergency—can create hardships for a business that may have a lasting impact on the relationship between employer and Reservist unless handled with diplomacy.

The better an employer understands Reserve obligations and the more a Reservist has helped prepare a business for his or her absence, the less likely will be an adverse affect when the period of mobilization is ended and employment is resumed. Indeed, a Reservist may forfeit reemployment rights by failing to request time off prior to an absence required for Reserve duties.

Reservists are protected from firing or discrimination because of military service; but they must take certain actions to guarantee protection of a civilian job, and other actions *should* be taken to help protect reemployment rights. Reserve commanders provide detailed information to members of their units in this regard.

The foregoing information relates to members of the Reserve and the National Guard mobilized under federal law; in the case of members of the National Guard called to active service by state governors, certain employment safeguards also apply. Regulations concerning them are made available to members of the Army National Guard and Air National Guard by unit commanders.

Employer Support

For Reserve and National Guard members who experience difficulties with employers relative to their Reserve training or with reemployment following mobilization, support is available from the Department of Defense, including the department's National Committee for Employer Support of the Guard and Reserve. That organization works continuously with private industry and the public to develop a thorough understanding of the country's military requirements and the importance of its Reserve components.

A Reservist's right to attend initial active duty training, inactive duty training (two days of drills per month), annual training duty, active duty for training, or extended active duty is protected by federal regulations. The law applies to all permanent employees, whether full-time or part-time, of private businesses or of federal, state, or local government agencies. The civilian job rights of Reservists who are temporary employees are not covered by the federal government.

Full- and part-time employees must request time off for military duties in order to be protected under the federal regulations. Failing to notify the employer in advance of a requirement to attend Reserve training or duty with the active forces can result in forfeiture of reemployment rights. An employer is required to permit participation in military training or active duty, but the Reservist must first request permission to do so.

In most instances, a Reservist cannot be required to forfeit vacation time for time spent at Reserve training or on active duty. If, however, an employer has a set vacation period during which work facilities are closed, the Reservist may have to give up some or all of vacation time if the vacation period and dates of Reserve training coincide. Additionally, if vacation time is based on years of employment, a business must continue to add to a Reservist's vacation time regardless of days spent at military training or on active duty.

Under laws protecting civilian job rights, there is no limit on the amount of time or the number of times a Reservist may be away from work for military training. To qualify for protection under law, a Reservist must report back to the place of employment on the first day following completion of training, plus the time required to return home from the training site.

Employees of civilian businesses or government agencies may not be discriminated against because of military service, and they retain their seniority rights. Until 1986, when a law was signed to strengthen Reserve job rights, an employer could refuse to hire someone who was in the Reserve forces. Such discrimination did not happen often but sometimes occurred in small businesses where employers determined that employee absences or scheduling problems related to Reserve service might lead to financial losses.

For a Reservist injured during military duty, an employer is required to assign the person to a new position with the same seniority and benefits as previously held—if such a job exists.

Employers do not have to reschedule work that someone misses because of Reserve duty; many companies do, however, and some even count an employee's Reserve duty as time worked for the company, for pay purposes. Historically, most business owners in the United States have supported employees who are members of the Reserve forces.

The National Committee for Employer Support of the Guard and Reserve monitors trends in civilian employer attitudes toward Reserve service and works toward improving employer support. The committee conducts a wide range of information and assistance programs to gain the attention of employers and develop and sustain their support. The committee has national headquarters just outside Washington in northern Virginia and is supported by smaller volunteer committees at more than fifty locations around the nation.

The national organization and its state committees establish and maintain contacts with business owners and community leaders to explain the significance of the Guard and Reserve. Speakers are provided to appear before influential employer audiences such as Chambers of Commerce and at meetings and conventions of other business-related groups. The Committee produces advertising campaigns, including direct-mail programs, to encourage employer support and presents awards to employers who enact personnel procedures that are supportive of Guard and Reserve service.

One of the most important services of the National Committee has been establishment of an ombudsman program to answer questions and help employers and employees understand the sometimes complex federal and state laws that cover service in the Guard and Reserve. In addition to an office at the Committee's national headquarters, ombudsman support also comes at the state level from trained volunteers. Some of the volunteers are attorneys and labor relations experts who have become thoroughly familiar with military issues and with federal and state regulations relating to Reserve service. The names and addresses of these experts and of state committee chairmen are available to Reservists and their employers from local Guard and Reserve training center offices throughout the country.

Among the main benefits of establishing a program such as Employer Support of the Guard and Reserve is in letting Reservists and those interested in Reserve service know that they are not alone if they encounter employment-related difficulties as a result of military duty. Much has been said and written over the years regarding morale among military forces and its overall importance in developing and maintaining strong units. Such discussions are often centered on active forces and overlook the critical nature of morale in fielding effective Reserve units. Since its establishment in 1972, the National Committee for Employer Support of the Guard and Reserve has been of direct benefit to morale among Reserve forces and contributed to mobilization readiness by enlisting the support of hundreds of thousands of business owners and managers.

Family Support

Until now, in discussing Reservists and their families, we have emphasized the need for keeping family members apprised of Reserve training procedures and requirements. At the same time, it is important for family members to support Reservists by helping to assure that personal affairs are in order at all times and by learning how to function in the event of a sudden and prolonged absence of the service member.

By informing family members of routine Reserve training activities and requirements, Reservists help build a base upon which family members can better function in the event of mobilization. Many Reserve units plan and organize activities in which families may gather for social events or simply to receive orientations relating to unit activities. By attending such functions and keeping up on unit schedules and administrative requirements, spouses and other family members can gain a clearer understanding of the Reserve service process and thereby assure their own well-being should Reservists be suddenly called to active duty.

Reserve service is, by its very nature, a commitment to readiness. A member of the Reserve forces takes on an obligation to be prepared to respond quickly and effectively to national or international crises or to local emergencies that pose a threat to the community. In order to meet that obligation, a Reservist must balance his or her military duty, civilian career, and family life in such a way that the three are consistently mutually supportive.

Chapter XI

Reserve Pay, Retirement Income, and Other Benefits

Often, young people examining the possibilities of service in the active armed forces or the Reserves consider only current military pay scales and choices of occupational fields before making their decision. The tendency is to look only toward the immediate goal—a well-paying job in which skills may be developed that will be useful both in the military and in civilian life.

Military service, however, has much more to offer. The benefits—beyond basic pay and occupational skills development—are substantial, regardless of whether an individual selects active or Reserve service and serves for only a few years or for a career of twenty or more years.

When a person enters Reserve service, the period of initial active duty varies among the Armed Forces and depends largely on the program chosen by the individual. Initial active duty for training is generally six months for enlisted members, whereas persons entering commissioning programs are usually required to serve with the active forces for two or more years.

During this initial active service, Reserve officers and enlisted personnel receive the same basic pay and allowances as do members of the active forces. Basic pay is based on rank and length of service. On military pay charts, ranks are categorized as officer (O) and enlisted (E). A number following the letter indicates the level of rank. For example, the pay grade O-4 represents the rank of major in the Army, Air Force, and

Marine Corps, or lieutenant commander in the Navy or Coast Guard.

The base pay for all individuals in each pay grade is the same in all the services. But, in addition to base pay, time in service and other factors must also be computed to determine what an individual will be paid each month. Pay increases are granted within pay grades based on length of service; and a service member may qualify for special pay such as flight pay or pay for serving as an active parachutist. Additionally, married members of the armed forces and some qualifying unmarried members, including Reservists on annual training duty, receive a monthly allowance for quarters (housing). An enlisted Reservist in the grade of E-4 receives a quarters allowance of just over $140 for a two-week period of annual training duty.

Drill Pay

After their initial active duty, Reservists attend weekend drills, which are called "inactive duty for training" and earn entitlement to the same pay members of the active forces are entitled to on a "per-day" basis—with one major difference. Reservists are paid the equivalent of one day of pay for each drill period they satisfactorily complete; however, a day of inactive duty for training is computed as two drill periods. Therefore, a Reservist performing two days of duty over a weekend, or at some other time during a month, is paid the equivalent of four days' pay in the amount prescribed by law for his or her pay grade and length of service. A corporal (pay grade E-4) in the Marine Corps Reserve with more than four, but less than six, years of service and not entitled to hazardous duty or other special pay, for example, would receive pay of $34.71 per drill; with four drills over the two days of a drill weekend, the corporal's total pay for the weekend is $138.85. (Four times $34.71 equals $138.84, but intricacies of the military pay system result in the corporal's receiving a penny more than that total.)

If that same corporal is not promoted to sergeant (pay grade

E-5) by the time he or she has completed six years of service, the basic pay will be increased to $36.08 per drill period and $144.32 for a weekend in which four drills are performed. Promotion to sergeant before reaching the sixth year of service would mean an increase in basic pay to $36.79 per drill period and a total of $147.17 for a weekend in which four drills were performed.

For the general public, the word "drill" is normally used to indicate the practice of some standard procedure, as in a "fire drill" or in the practice of certain plays by an athletic team in preparation for a game. For Reserve service purposes, however, the term "drill" does not necessarily mean practice of standardized procedures during a drill period or weekend. The Reservist or unit may indeed practice some standard military procedures, ranging from ceremonial functions to battle tactics; but more often than not, a drill weekend consists of a series of different activities.

Some of those activities may well be practice of specific procedures, but others may include classes on military subjects, maintenance of equipment, written or on-the-job testing, or a number of other activities that are routine military requirements. In some instances, Reservists take part in operational activities in support of active force missions.

For many units, a typical drill weekend consists of a Saturday morning muster in which Reservists arrive at the training center, attend roll call, and are briefed on activities planned for the weekend. Following muster they proceed to assigned tasks until the lunch hour, which may involve food delivered to the unit, a meal at a military dining facility, or a meal of special rations designed for use in field training and combat operations. After lunch, Reservists return to their assigned duties until late afternoon. If weekend training does not include field activities, Reservists are often dismissed for the evening and may go home for the night. Whether they remain at the training center overnight, are in the field, or return the next morning, members of a unit attend roll call at a specified time on Sunday morning and complete the second day of their monthly training requirement.

The nature of a Reserve unit, its mission, or other consid-erations may result in Reservists completing monthly drills at times other than on a weekend or with their entire unit present. Each Reservist is, however, required by law to complete 48 drill periods, or the equivalent of 12 drill weekends, each year, as well as two weeks of annual training duty.

Pay for the two weeks of annual training duty is computed at the same rate as for members of the active forces.

Other Benefits

Beyond the basic pay received for drills and annual training duty, Reservists receive a number of other important bene-fits—and in some instances special pay.

By federal law, Reservists qualify for benefits based on their active duty service and their inactive duty for training drill periods. If they serve until retirement, they qualify for certain benefits for the period between retirement from Reserve ser-vice and the time they reach age sixty; and they receive other benefits at age sixty and beyond.

When a Reservist first enters service and is undergoing the initial period of active duty training, during the two weeks of annual training duty, and at other times when serving on active duty (other than on drill weekends), benefits are generally the same as for members of the active forces. Among these are use of military exchanges, commissaries and clubs; certain amounts and types of medical and dental care; access to military recrea-tional and entertainment activities; legal assistance; access to flights on military aircraft for certain types of personal travel within the United States; life insurance; and certain benefits conveyed in the event of the death of the Reservist.

After a Reservist has completed the initial period of active service and is in inactive duty drill status (and obligated to attend drill periods at a training center near home), some of those same benefits, as well as others, apply. The Reservist is eligible for full-time Serviceman's Group Life Insurance; mili-tary exchange privileges based on each drill period attended per month; medical care for injuries that occur while traveling to and from drills and during drills; access to military clothing stores, clubs, theaters, and temporary lodging facilities on military bases (when available and it does not interfere with the lodging of members of the active forces); space-available air transportation within the U.S. and Puerto Rico; certain survivor benefits in the event of the death of the Reservist; and Veterans Administration medical and dental benefits if injured while performing military duties.

Use of military base exchanges, which are similar to civilian department and variety stores (but generally with lower prices), is conveyed to a Reservist and his or her dependents at the rate of one day's use for each drill period performed; thus, for a drill weekend, the privilege of using an exchange is conveyed for any four days during the month. The Reservist and dependents must possess proper military or military-dependent identification. Use of a military commissary, a form of grocery store with most items priced substantially lower than at civilian stores, is conveyed to Reservists at a rate of one day for each day of active duty served during each year.

Reservists who become ill or are injured while engaged in Reserve duty are usually eligible for medical treatment and, if needed, hospitalization paid for by the government. If the illness or injury causes disability and occurs while the Reservist is on active duty for more than thirty days, the individual may qualify for disability pay and allowances. A Reservist who is found to have been disabled in the line of duty while on active duty for training or during a drill period may qualify for disability pay and allowances; however, funds received for civilian employment will be considered in possibly reducing the amount of military disability payments.

Serviceman's Group Life Insurance is available to Reservists at very low costs for coverage up to $50,000. Reservists suffering injuries in the line of duty that cause them to be uninsurable at standard insurance rates may apply for Veterans Group Life Insurance in amounts up to $50,000. Reservists qualifying for retirement may also participate in the Reserve Component Survivor Benefit Plan, under which a number of options are available by which a member shares the cost of a program that results in monthly payments to certain survivors. Reservists are required to participate in the federal Social Security program; therefore, Federal Insurance Contribution Act (FICA) contributions are withheld from base pay.

The spouse or other member of the family is entitled to a death gratuity payment and burial expenses, up to certain limits, should the Reservist die while on active duty or die as a result of service-connected causes within 120 days after such training. If death should occur as a result of injury during a period of inactive duty for training—a weekend drill—a death gratuity is paid if the death is within 120 days. The military death gratuity payment is an amount based on the pay grade of the deceased Reservist and any incentive or hazardous duty pay times six; in other words, the family member receiving the gratuity would receive the equivalent of six months of base pay and special pay.

If a Reservist dies while on active duty or active duty for training—and sometimes during an inactive duty for training (drill) period—or from a service-connected disability following such service, certain surviving family members are entitled to military dependency and indemnity compensation. This compensation may be paid to a surviving spouse, children under eighteen (or children up to age twenty-three if they are attending school), or, in some instances, to surviving parents. Dependency and indemnity compensation is not reduced as a result of any Social Security payments made to the survivors of Reservists.

Amounts of dependency and indemnity compensation are based on the deceased individual's highest pay grade while on active duty and can amount to a substantial income to survivors over a period of years. At the time of writing the unremarried spouse of an enlisted Reservist in the pay grade E-5 who qualified for dependency and indemnity compensation would receive $622 per month; the spouse of an officer in grade O-5 would receive $879 per month. Upon remarrying, the surviving spouse's compensation would be terminated but could be reinstated in the event the new marriage partner died or the marriage were otherwise legally terminated.

Each unmarried child of a deceased service member covered by dependency indemnity compensation and who is under the age of eighteen—or qualified for compensation up to age twenty-three while attending school—also receives monthly payments. The amount of the payment at the time of writing was $83 per month unless the deceased service member had no surviving spouse. With no surviving spouse, the monthly rate of compensation would increase, with the amount of payment determined by the number of surviving children. In most instances, dependency and indemnity compensation to children ends when they reach eighteen; however, payments may be made and continued for children over eighteen when they are physically or mentally disabled.

The Department of Veterans Affairs may provide Reservists with compensation, hospitalization, outpatient medical and dental care, and other health-related benefits for disease or injuries incurred or aggravated in the line of duty. In certain instances, Department of Veterans Affairs burial benefits are also conveyed to Reservists. In some circumstances, the types and amounts of active duty performed by Reservists or service-connected disabilities make them eligible for Department of Veterans Affairs home mortgage loans and other types of loans.

Retirement Benefits

Many Reservists continue their service beyond the period for which they contracted to serve and eventually qualify for retirement benefits. After completing twenty or more years of military service (which may be a combination of active and Reserve service), and transferring to the Retired Reserve prior to reaching age sixty, a Reservist temporarily loses some of the preretirement benefits until reaching age sixty. At age sixty, the retired Reservist becomes eligible for retired pay, certain of the benefits that were available before retirement, and some benefits that had been available only on a limited basis while in inactive duty drill status. Among the benefits lost while in a retired status and prior to age sixty are exchange and commissary privileges, medical and dental care, military legal assistance, and use of base recreational facilities.

During the period between Reserve retirement and reaching age sixty, the individual may still use base clubs, if permitted to do so by individual base regulations; fly aboard military aircraft for certain types of personal trips if space is available; and continue participation in the Serviceman's Group Life Insurance program. They may also wear their military uniforms on certain occasions.

When a retired Reservist reaches age sixty he or she becomes eligible to apply for retired pay, which is paid on a monthly basis and is mailed to the individual or sent to a financial institution through a direct deposit program.

In certain circumstances Reservists eligible for retired pay may choose not to receive all of the money they are entitled to each month or may choose not to receive any of it and use only other Reserve retirement benefits. Usually Reservists choosing this course do so because they may be eligible to receive their choice of either retired pay or a Department of Veterans Affairs pension or other compensation that is exempt from Federal taxes; retired Reserve pay is not exempt.

Retired Reservists over age sixty are eligible for medical care for themselves and their dependents at military medical facilities, dental care for themselves and limited dental care for their dependents at military facilities, and they may participate in civilian medical care programs in which the federal government pays substantial portions of costs.

Another important benefit to retired Reservists over age sixty is unlimited use of base exchanges and commissaries for themselves and their dependents. That benefit, over the course of several years, can save thousands of dollars in the purchase of food and other essentials. Among other benefits for retirees after age sixty are eligibility for use of Veterans Administration hospitals, legal services, military air transportation for themselves and their dependents when space is available, base veterinary facilities, and base clubs and recreational facilities.

Retired Reservists may continue participation in the Serviceman's Group Life Insurance program up to the maximum amount of $50,000, but eligibility ceases at age sixty.

Tangibles and Intangibles

The benefits available to members of the armed forces, including Reservists, change somewhat from year to year but usually only slightly. Therefore, it is important for anyone considering Reserve service to discuss with recruiters all of the benefits available at present.

It is also important to examine the value of each benefit. Some—such as basic pay and allowances—can be easily measured and evaluated relative to an individual's life-style and plans for the future. Not all benefits, however, are tangible, and the value of many cannot be easily assessed by a young person just embarking on adulthood. Among intangible benefits, for example, are the camaraderie and personal relationships that usually evolve during Reserve service. Also difficult to measure is the positive impact that military service often has on personal growth, maturity, and development as a leader.

It is also important to look at benefits not only individually but in total as well. Someone considering Reserve service and interested in receiving specialized training of importance in development of civilian career plans may have a tendency to overlook other benefits.

For the young man or woman looking into Reserve service, it is wise to prepare a written list of benefits and discuss them with military recruiters and family members. Such a study will provide a better perspective of the overall value of Reserve service. The list should cover pay, insurance, retirement programs, leadership experience, military specialty training, education programs such as the Reserve G.I. bill, associations with other members of the community, travel, reemployment rights, post exchange and commissary privileges, and any other benefits available at the time Reserve service is being considered.

Many people who join the Reserve forces find that the total experience of service as a citizen-soldier is the most important benefit they gain from military duty. Pay, allowances, first-rate training, and new skills—combined with the satisfaction that comes from service to one's country—can have a very positive lifelong impact on the person who commits to service with the Reserve forces.

Chapter XII

Education and Opportunity

In the preceding chapter, we looked at some of the many benefits provided to members of the Reserve forces and noted that some are intangible. For the most part, those examined are clearly tangible forms of payment or rewards for military service. One of the most significant is education.

Another benefit at first glance may seem to be intangible and doesn't show up on charts at all. That benefit is equal opportunity in one of its most refined forms. In combination, education and equal opportunity are among the most important of all benefits accrued by military service.

Anyone successfully completing a period of service, either as a member of the active armed forces or as a Reservist, is usually highly skilled in his or her military specialty. And often the specialty is one that can be carried over to civilian applications. Many older Americans believe that skills learned in military jobs and through education under the G.I. Bill enabled World War II veterans—many of whom were Reservists—to help establish the strong business and industrial base enjoyed by this country in the years following the war.

Although it is sometimes hard to relate some military skills— such as infantry specialties—directly to civilian applications, the long hours of study and training that lead to proficiency with infantry weapons do help instill in a person the discipline and attention to detail needed to study and master civilian occupational fields. Additionally, it should be remembered that for every military occupational specialty relating directly to combat operations, many others exist to support the combat specialties. That means there is a continual need for extremely proficient specialists in administrative and technical fields. Computer programmers, electronic equipment repair personnel, inventory and distribution specialists, aviation repair technicians, automotive mechanics, communications equipment operators—specialists in these and hundreds of other types of jobs are needed to assure mobilization readiness.

For the young man or woman interested in Reserve service, the choice of specialties available generally relates to the type of Reserve unit or units in the community. Available positions and the test scores achieved on examinations administered by the armed forces help determine assignments. The tests are used for a number of purposes, including determination of aptitude and potential for acquiring specific skills.

When someone entering Reserve service is found qualified to enter training in a specific field—and a need exists within a local Reserve unit for that specialty—the recruit attends basic training before receiving specialty instruction. Often the person moves directly from basic training to a service school for formal specialty training. In some instances, training is achieved on the job with units of the active force before the Reservist returns to the local unit. Throughout a Reservist's service, training continues during weekend drills and at annual training duty. Additionally, Reservists may be assigned to extended active duty to attend formal service schools in order to upgrade current skills or gain new ones.

Few employers place as much emphasis on education as does the Department of Defense. This is reflected in the number of high school graduates among military personnel; today, nearly all enlistees in the services are high school graduates. The relatively few who are not have demonstrated through testing that they possess the requisite learning skills to do well in armed forces training programs and schools.

Basic Training

The Army and Air Force refer to "basic"; sailors and Marines sometimes call it "boot camp." What they are talking about is basic training, the period of initial service in which a person is introduced to his or her service and learns the basic aspects of military life. Instruction is received in service history and traditions, military customs and courtesy, military justice, proper wear and care of military uniforms, teamwork, and other areas that help to provide a common base on which to build a military career—regardless of the length of that career.

Each of the services has its own type of basic training, which is aimed at developing teamwork, establishing an understanding of the needs and objectives of the service, and developing the level of physical fitness needed to operate with other members of the force. For example, for Marines—active and Reserve—basic training is the initial stage of what is now called "basic warrior training." It is designed to develop in each male Marine the skills needed to perform as part of a frontline combat unit—regardless of his military occupational specialty—should need arise for additional frontline troops in a tactical situation.

For all of the services, basic training is a time of orientation and familiarization, a point of departure designed to put everyone on equal footing as they begin their military service.

Specialty Training

Following basic training, many Reservists have the opportunity to take specialty training in service-operated schools located at bases throughout the U.S. Formal specialty training for personnel from all of the armed forces may be operated at one location in facilities provided by one of the services. Formal military training in journalism, for example, is conducted at a joint service school at the Army's Fort Benjamin Harrison in Indiana. Each of the armed forces is represented on the staff at the school, and classes usually include personnel from each of the services. Like the formal courses of other service schools, the journalism courses at Fort Benjamin Harrison range from basic to advanced.

Many advanced training courses at formal schools last from eight to twelve weeks. If the time available following basic training and before a Reservist is scheduled to return to his home Reserve unit does not permit attendance at a formal school, he or she may be assigned to an active force unit for a period of on-the-job training. In such cases, as a Reservist progresses at the local unit, opportunities may arise later for attendance at formal schools.

Regardless of the specialty, courses of instruction at formal military schools are often among the best available anywhere. Some colleges confer credits for completion of such courses. Instruction is usually a combination of classroom work, laboratory work, and practical application.

In each of the more than 250 military occupational specialties available to Army Reservists, a number of soldiers have risen to the top of their field. It is from among these individuals that instructors are usually chosen for the staffs of formal service schools. The same holds true for each of the armed forces. The result is some of the best instruction available anywhere.

Sometimes skills needed by the Reserve components may lead to unusual opportunities for individuals to receive very specialized instruction at government expense. Two examples are language and medical programs. The Army Defense Language Institute, for example, was created to develop proficiency in a wide range of languages. The instruction is intense and considered among the best in the world; completion of a language course through the Institute is often worth college credits, since many schools recognize the high level of instruction it provides.

The Naval Reserve helps assure the availability of specially trained medical technicians for the Navy through the Naval Reserve Allied Medical Personnel Program. It is designed to allow individuals to complete training in a medical field at a civilian college or technical school while serving as Reservists. Persons qualifying may receive payment for full tuition, books, and required fees from the Naval Reserve. Participants in the program are obligated to six years of weekend drills and annual training duty, plus two more years in an inactive Reserve status. Some of the eleven types of medical specialists who evolve from the program: advanced ocular technicians, advanced X-ray technicians, biomedical equipment technicians, and operating room technicians.

Many business success stories are told in which members of the Reserve and National Guard learned and refined skills in military specialties, transferred the knowledge and skills to the civilian workplace, and developed profitable companies. Of all the opportunities provided by the armed forces, military occupational skills training is among the most important.

Professional Development

In each of the armed forces, professional development educational programs help assure that as senior members of the active and Reserve forces complete their careers, other qualified members are prepared to move up and assume positions of leadership—positions comparable to senior executive levels in the civilian community. For the enlisted ranks, schools have been developed by each of the services to prepare soldiers, sailors, airmen, and Marines for increased responsibility and leadership. At the officer level, general development and leadership schools may be attended as an officer progresses up the leadership chain. Completion of such schools—and class standing at graduation—are important factors in promotion to the next higher grade.

Additionally, off-duty correspondence courses and other special educational programs have been developed by the services to assist in professional development and occupational skills proficiency. Reservists are encouraged to take advantage of such programs to improve technical and general military knowledge and capabilities.

Professional development programs may cover military science, engineering, health sciences, management, or any of several other fields—or combinations of fields—and may include work not only at military schools but at civilian institutions of higher learning.

Civilian Education

In recent years the armed forces have benefited from a number of initiatives that have opened opportunities for Reservists to pursue college degrees or obtain vocational and technical training. The most important of the current programs is the Montgomery G.I. Bill, named for a member of Congress who was instrumental in creating the legislation needed for the program.

Under the bill, Reservists may be eligible for benefits of more than $5,000, which can be applied to their education while they are attending classes.

Another program available to some Reservists attending college provides up to 75 percent of tuition for approved courses. Under both programs, a Reservist who completes initial active duty for training and enrolls in an approved college program receives a check each month to apply toward college costs. Full-time students may qualify for $140 per month for up to 36 months; students attending school on other than a full-time basis may also qualify for reduced levels of education assistance funds.

Other programs are available to assist those who seek college degrees. A Reservist who has or plans to apply for a federally guaranteed student loan, National Direct Student Loan, or Federally Insured Student Loan can receive assistance from the Reserve component in repaying the debt. For each year of Reserve service, 15 percent of the loan or $500—whichever is greater—will be repaid, up to a total of $10,000. After six years of Reserve service, a substantial portion of a Reservist's college loan could be paid off through the program.

Each of the services has education-related programs that can be described in detail by recruiters. As with all other service-related programs, detailed information should be sought and assurances obtained regarding an applicant's qualifications to receive such educational assistance.

ROTC Programs

Among the most widely known educational opportunities offered by the armed forces are the Reserve Officer Training Corps programs of the Army, Navy, and Air Force (persons interested in Marine Corps service may apply for "Marine Option" status within the Naval ROTC program). The ROTC programs produce the majority of the armed forces' commissioned officers. More than 500 Army, Navy, and Air Force ROTC units exist in private and public colleges and universities around the nation; through cross-enrollments and other agreements, the ROTC program extends to more than 2,000 campuses.

Those successfully completing an ROTC program are commissioned as armed forces Reserve officers upon graduation from college.

Curriculum for ROTC components at colleges and universities consists of leadership and management training courses, which are presented a few hours each week. Participants may qualify for full tuition scholarships, which may also cover other fees such as the costs of books, supplies, and equipment. Additionally, it is sometimes possible to qualify for a tax-free allowance of up to $1,000 each year the scholarship is in effect.

Upon completion of their education, ROTC participants are often commissioned during college or university commencement ceremonies and immediately begin serving on active duty or in the National Guard. For those entering active service, upon completion of an initial period of active duty—which usually lasts two to four years—they remain members of the Reserve forces for an additional period. This may be with an organized Reserve unit in or near their home community, or it may be in a status in which they are not required to attend drills but may be subject to call in the event of mobilization.

Equal Opportunity

The training and education programs in the active and Reserve forces are major elements in another type of benefit that is often unlisted on military service benefit charts. That benefit is equal opportunity.

For many young people today, the extremely high cost of living that is prevalent in most parts of the country makes it difficult to make ends meet for them and their families. As a result, it is often impractical or impossible to pursue college or vocational courses without extreme sacrifice.

Through programs available to all members of the armed forces—active and Reserve—opportunities are opened that may lead to better jobs and a general improvement in life-style. And these opportunities are available to all. Among all segments of society, the armed forces have been among the leading insitutions in establishing procedures designed to assure equal opportunity for women, minorities, and persons from economically depressed families.

One of the most important aspects of military service is teamwork. Today's military leaders recognize that to have efficient, effective, hard-working, and well-organized teams, every member must have the same opportunities to learn, to train, and to advance. To assure that this happens, the Department of Defense has set in place an aggressive equal opportunity program that is closely monitored at the highest levels of leadership.

In civilian businesses the matter of equal pay for equal performance has been difficult to gauge and, therefore, difficult to control. In the military, however, equality in the selection of personnel for advancement, for special training, and for placement in leadership positions can be effectively monitored and has become an important part of the overall evaluation and inspection of military units at all levels. As a result, many of today's enlisted personnel and officers in senior positions of responsibility within the active and Reserve forces are women and minorities.

As stated at the beginning of this chapter, the combination of education and equal opportunity is among the most important of all benefits conveyed to persons entering military service. Taking advantage of the two leads to almost limitless career advancement possibilities, either as a Reservist or as a member of the active forces.

Consider this: The senior military officer among all men and women in the U.S. Armed Forces is the Chairman of the Joint Chiefs of Staff. Of the last three men selected to be Chairman of the Joint Chiefs of Staff, one entered military service as an enlisted member of the Army National Guard; another is a black man—the son of immigrants.

Members of the Reserve forces are encouraged to set their sights high. Those who do aim for high goals and work hard to attain their professional objectives can expect to be supported by a very effective system.

Appendix A

Annual Earnings—Enlisted Reservists

Enlisted Reservists are paid monthly for drill periods, which usually are conducted one weekend per month. Pay is earned on the basis of two drills per day, four drills per two-day training period. A Reservist's pay for one drill is the equivalent of the amount a member of the active forces of the same rank and time in service would receive for one day. Therefore, in effect, a Reservist receives four days' pay for two days of drills. Annual pay also includes money received for the 14-day period of annual training duty required of Reservists; pay for annual training duty is computed at the same daily rate as for members of the active forces. The following table reflects basic pay (rounded to the nearest dollar) that would be received by a Reservist attending 12 weekend training periods (48 drills) and a 14-day stint of annual training duty. (The table does not reflect basic allowance for subsistence or for quarters, or special pay received by parachutists and certain others. Monthly pay for grade E-1 is $1389 during the first four months of service.)

Enlisted Reserve Pay

Years of Service / Pay Grade	2 or less	Over 2	Over 3	Over 4	Over 6	Over 8	Over 10	Over 12	Over 14	Over 16	Over 18	Over 20	Over 22	Over 26
E-9	—	—	—	—	—	—	4331	4430	4530	4779	4731	4830	5084	5578
E-8	—	—	—	—	—	3633	3736	3834	3935	4039	4132	4237	4482	4982
E-7	$2536	2738	2840	2939	3040	3136	3237	3337	3488	3587	3688	3736	3795	4482
E-6	2182	2379	2478	2584	2679	2777	2879	3027	3122	3223	3272	3272	3272	3272
E-5	1915	2085	2186	2281	2430	2529	2630	2727	2777	2777	2777	2777	2777	2777
E-4	1787	1892	1997	2152	2237	2237	2237	2237	2237	2237	2237	2237	2237	2237
E-3	1683	1775	1805	1920	1920	1920	1920	1920	1920	1920	1920	1920	1920	1920
E-2	1619	1619	1619	1619	1619	1619	1619	1619	1619	1619	1619	1619	1619	1619
E-1	1444	1444	1444	1444	1444	1444	1444	1444	1444	1444	1444	1444	1444	1444

Appendix **B**

Annual Earnings—Reserve Officers

Reserve officers are paid monthly for drill periods, which usually are conducted one weekend per month. Pay is earned on the basis of two drills per day, four drills per two-day training period. A Reservist's pay for one drill is the equivalent of the amount a member of the active forces of the same rank and time in service would receive for one day. Therefore, in effect, a Reservist receives four days' pay for two days of drills. Annual pay also includes money received for the 14-day period of annual training duty required of Reservists; pay for annual training duty is computed at the same daily rate as for members of the active forces. The following table reflects basic pay (rounded to the nearest dollar) which would be received by a Reservist attending 12 weekend training periods (48 drills) and a 14-day stint of annual training duty. (The table does not reflect basic allowances for subsistence or quarters or special pay received by pilots, parachutists, and certain others. Officers who have served four years of active service as enlisted personnel receive more pay than officers who have not. Pay scales for those officers and for warrant officers are available from armed forces recruiters.)

Reserve Officer Pay

Years of Service / Pay Grade	2 Or less	Over 2	Over 3	Over 4	Over 6	Over 8	Over 10	Over 12	Over 14	Over 16	Over 18	Over 20	Over 22	Over 26
O-8	9530	9814	10045	10045	10790	10790	10790	11297	11297	11765	12273	12742	13250	13250
O-7	7928	8463	8463	8463	8785	8785	9350	9350	9814	10790	11528	11528	11528	11528
O-6	5891	6416	6887	6887	6887	6887	6887	6887	7118	8235	8654	8840	9350	10135
O-5	4723	5536	5914	5914	5914	5914	6093	6417	6842	7350	7770	8002	8270	8270
O-4	3989	4845	5166	5166	5259	5490	5860	6187	6467	6748	6933	6933	6933	6933
O-3	3712	4142	4424	4890	5121	5304	5586	5860	6003	6003	6003	6003	6003	6003
O-2	3243	3537	4237	4378	4469	4469	4469	4469	4469	4469	4469	4469	4469	4469
O-1	2879	2937	3537	3537	3537	3537	3537	3537	3537	3537	3537	3537	3537	3537

Appendix C

Reserve Information Sources

In addition to local armed forces recruiting personnel, the following may also provide information helpful to those considering Reserve service:

Reserve Officers Association of the United States
1 Constitution Avenue NE
Washington, DC 20002

Naval Reserve Association
1619 King Street
Alexandria, VA 22314

Marine Corps Reserve Officers Association
201 North Washington Street
Alexandria, VA 22314

Naval Enlisted Reserve Association
6703 Farragut Avenue
Falls Church, VA 22042

The Fleet Reserve Association
1303 New Hampshire Avenue NW
Washington, DC

Enlisted Association of the National Guard
  of the United States
One Massachusetts Avenue NW
Washington, DC 20001

National Guard Association of the United States
1 Massachusetts Avenue NW
Washington, DC 20001

Index